# The TKT
**Teaching Knowledge Test**
# Course

Mary Spratt

Alan Pulverness

Melanie Williams

*Published in collaboration with Cambridge ESOL*

UNIVERSITY *of* CAMBRIDGE
ESOL Examinations

**English for Speakers of Other Languages**

CAMBRIDGE
UNIVERSITY PRESS

CAMBRIDGE UNIVERSITY PRESS

Cambridge, New York, Melbourne, Madrid, Cape Town, Singapore, São Paulo, Delhi

Cambridge University Press
The Edinburgh Building, Cambridge CB2 8RU, UK

www.cambridge.org
Information on this title: www.cambridge.org/9780521609920

First published 2005
6th printing 2008

Printed in the United Kingdom at the University Press, Cambridge

*A catalogue record for this publication is available from the British Library*

ISBN 978-0-521-60992-0 paperback

# Contents

# Introduction

## What is the Teaching Knowledge Test (TKT)?

The Teaching Knowledge Test (TKT) is a test developed by Cambridge ESOL for teachers of English to speakers of other languages. TKT tests candidates' knowledge of concepts related to language, language use and the background to and practice of language teaching and learning. It is not a test of the practical skills teachers need to use in their own classrooms or of English language proficiency.

TKT consists of three modules which can be taken together, or separately, in any order. The content of TKT is tested by means of objective tasks, such as matching and multiple choice. The test for each module consists of 80 questions.

There are no entry requirements for TKT, such as previous teaching experience and/or teaching or language qualifications, but candidates should have at least an intermediate level of English, e.g. PET, IELTS 4, CEF / ALTE B1. They are also expected to understand a range of about 400 terms describing the practice of English Language Teaching (ELT). A selection of these terms appears in each TKT module. A list of the terms that may occur in TKT is provided in the *TKT Glossary* which is on the Cambridge ESOL website: http://www.cambridgeesol.org/TKT.

Candidates are encouraged to keep a teaching portfolio to help them reflect on their teaching practice, but this portfolio is not assessed.

## What is *The TKT Course*?

*The TKT Course* has four main aims:
1  To introduce readers to the concepts and terms about teaching and learning that are central to TKT, and to give them opportunities to do exam practice with TKT sample test tasks and exam papers.
2  To introduce readers to the main current theories, approaches and activities in ELT and assess their usefulness for the classroom.
3  To share with readers some of the many resources available to English language teachers.
4  To provide materials and activities that give teachers opportunities for professional development by exploring the concepts which have been introduced.

## Who is *The TKT Course* written for?

*The TKT Course* is written for the following readers:
* Readers intending to take TKT. They may be studying for it on a course, or alone as self-access students.
* Readers following introductory teacher development courses in teaching English, or retraining to become English language teachers.
* Readers working by themselves to improve their knowledge of ELT.
* Readers who have not started teaching yet, and readers who are already teaching in primary or secondary schools.
* Both first and second language speakers of English.

The language used in *The TKT Course* is at the same level as the language used in TKT, i.e. intermediate level English at approximately IELTS band 4 or CEF (Common European Framework) B1.

The material in the book is designed to provide approximately 60–90 hours of study.

## What are the contents of *The TKT Course*?

The contents of *The TKT Course* follow the contents and order of the TKT specifications. The book contains:

- three modules, each focusing on one module of TKT. Each module is divided into units covering the contents of the TKT specifications for that module. The units focus on topics from the module, and then provide tasks and activities exploring the topics and preparing the reader for TKT.
- ELT terms from the *TKT Glossary*. These occur in each unit and are shown in **bold** the first time they appear in a unit. They are defined the first time they appear in the book and some are defined again later, if they have another meaning.
- three TKT practice tests, one for each module.
- exam tips for taking TKT.
- answer keys for the Follow-up activities, TKT practice tasks and TKT practice tests.
- two lists of the ELT terms from the *TKT Glossary* that are used in the book. The first list gives the terms for the whole book in alphabetical order, and the second gives the terms for each unit. The first list gives the page where each term is defined.

The units build on one another, so that the ideas introduced in one unit provide the foundation for the ideas introduced in the next unit. Similarly, each module provides a foundation for the next module, as in the design of TKT.

- Module 1 focuses on terms and concepts commonly used to describe language and language skills; the background to language learning; activities and approaches in ELT and assessment.
- Module 2 focuses on lesson planning and the use of resources and materials.
- Module 3 focuses on the language that teachers and learners use in the classroom and on techniques for classroom management.

## How is each unit organised and how can it be used?

The advice in the table opposite is intended for those using the book on a taught course or for self-access readers. It can also be adapted for use by trainers.

Each unit in *The TKT Course* follows the same structure:

| Section | Purpose | Suggestions for use |
|---|---|---|
| Starter question and answer | To provide a definition of the key terms in the title of the unit. | Try to answer the question before reading the answer. |
| Key concepts | To introduce the main ideas of the topic of the unit and to explain the key ELT terms. | There is a short question at the beginning of this section. Try answering it before reading the text that follows. This section could be read outside class. |
| Key concepts and the language teaching classroom | To discuss how the key concepts influence English language teaching and learning. | It would be useful to think about how each point might influence what you do in the classroom. |
| Follow-up activities | To allow the reader to work with the key concepts in order to understand them more fully. N.B. These activities do not use the same question formats as those used in TKT. | These activities are designed for use in or outside the classroom. Completing them leads to a much fuller understanding of the unit's key concepts. There is an answer key for these activities on pages 171–5. |
| Reflection | To encourage the reader to develop his/her opinions on the key concepts by considering questions or comments from teachers and learners. | Discuss these points with others if possible. As this section is about opinions, it does not have answers. |
| Discovery activities | To help the reader to find out more about the key concepts, to experiment with them in the classroom and to assess their usefulness. | These activities involve doing things outside the classroom, e.g. reading chapters from books, finding websites, seeing how key concepts are applied in coursebooks, trying out ideas in the classroom and writing comments in the TKT portfolio. N.B. Decide if it is more useful to write the TKT portfolio in English or your own language. |
| TKT practice task | To review the unit's content and to help readers become familiar with the TKT task formats and level. N.B. These tasks use the same question formats as those used in TKT. | Do this task to familiarise yourself with the formats of TKT and to test yourself on the contents of the unit. You can check your answers in the answer key on page 176. |

## Introduction

We suggest that readers using this book by themselves choose a coursebook to use for the Discovery activities and think of a specific group of learners for the Reflection and Discovery activities.

We also recommend readers to look at the *TKT Glossary* (http://www.cambridgeesol.org/TKT) as they work through the book, to help consolidate and extend understanding of ELT terms. It may also be useful to have a good dictionary near you, e.g. *Cambridge Advanced Learners' Dictionary*, Cambridge University Press 2003.

Enjoy your teaching and your reflection on your teaching, and good luck to those who take TKT.

# Language and background to language learning and teaching

## Part 1 | Describing language and language skills

### Unit 1 Grammar

## ▪ What is grammar?

Grammar describes how we combine, organise and change words and parts of words to make meaning. We use rules for this description.

## ▪ Key concepts

What are parts of speech, grammatical structures and word formation?

We can use grammar to describe parts of speech, grammatical structures and how words are formed.

There are nine parts of speech: nouns, verbs, adjectives, adverbs, determiners, prepositions, pronouns, conjunctions and exclamations. A **part of speech** or word class describes the function a word or phrase has in a sentence. This controls how the word or phrase can operate and combine grammatically with other words. For example, in English:

- a noun can act as the subject of a verb but an adjective cannot
  e.g. *The tall girl ran very fast* (✔) but not *Tall ran very fast* (✗)
- an adverb can combine with an adjective but an adjective cannot combine with another adjective
  e.g. *well organised* (✔), *good organised* (✗)
- a noun can combine with another noun
  e.g. *a car park*.

The table below shows the functions of the different parts of speech:

| Part of speech | Examples | Function(s) |
|---|---|---|
| **Nouns** (e.g. countable, uncountable) | *children*<br>*sugar* | • to name people, places, things, qualities, ideas, or activities<br>• to act as the subject/object of the verb |
| **Verbs** (e.g. transitive, intransitive) | *see*<br>*run* | • to show an action, state or experience |

| Part of speech | Examples | Function |
|---|---|---|
| **Adjectives** (e.g. comparative) | *easier* | • to describe or give more information about a noun, pronoun or part of a sentence |
| **Adverbs** (e.g. of degree, manner, time) | *completely* *quickly* *yesterday* | • to describe or give more information about how, when or where something happens<br>• to add information to adjectives, verbs, other adverbs or sentences |
| **Determiners** (e.g. possessive adjectives, articles, demonstrative adjectives, quantifiers) | *my* *the* *this* *both* | • to make clear which noun is referred to or to give information about quantity |
| **Prepositions** (e.g. of time, place, direction) | *after* *at* *towards* | • to connect a noun, noun phrase or pronoun to another word or phrase |
| **Pronouns** (e.g. personal, possessive, relative, reflexive) | *she* *mine* *who* *myself* | • to replace or refer to a noun or noun phrase just mentioned |
| **Conjunctions** (e.g. of reason, addition, contrast) | *as* *and* *but* | • to join words, sentences or parts of sentences |
| Exclamations (e.g. of doubt, pain) | *Er* *Ow* | • to show a (strong) feeling – especially in informal spoken language |

We can divide the parts of speech into further categories, e.g. countable and uncountable nouns and transitive and intransitive verbs.

Grammar rules also describe **grammatical structures**, i.e. the arrangement of words into patterns which have meaning. The rules for grammatical structures use grammatical terms to describe forms and uses. 'Form' refers to the specific grammatical parts that make up the structure and the order they occur in. 'Use' refers to the meaning that the structure is used to express. Look at these examples:

| Term | Form | Use |
|---|---|---|
| Past continuous tense | subject + past tense of verb *to be* + -*ing* form of verb e.g. *he was running* | • to describe a temporary or background situation or action in the past |
| Passive voice | subject + *to be* + past participle (+ *by* + agent) e.g. *the road was built (by the company)* | • to show what happens to people or things |
| Comparative of 'long' adjectives | *more* + long adjective (+ *than*) e.g. *he was more embarrassed than his friend* | • generally used with adjectives of two syllables or more to compare separate things or people |

We also use grammar to describe how words are formed. English uses **prefixes** (a group of letters added at the beginning of a word) and **suffixes** (a group of letters added at the end of a word) to create new words. The prefixes and suffixes are added to base words (e.g. *stop, book*) to make new grammatical units such as tenses, parts of verbs, the plural of nouns, possessives, e.g. *talked, goes, going, books, girl's*. Many other prefixes (e.g. *un-, il-, pre-, dis-*) and suffixes (e.g. *-tion, -est, -ly, -able*) are also used in English to make new words e.g. *disappear, careful, friendly*. Some languages, e.g. Turkish and German, make a lot of use of prefixes and suffixes to create new words. Other languages make little or no use of them.

Grammar includes a large number of terms, grammatical structures, uses and forms. This unit only introduces them generally. The *TKT Glossary* (http://www.cambridgeesol.org/TKT) and the grammar books and websites suggested in the Discovery activities on page 8 provide more information.

## Key concepts and the language teaching classroom

- Grammar rules describe the way that language works, but language changes over time, so grammar rules are not fixed. They change too. Unfortunately, grammar rules and grammar books don't always change as quickly as the language, so they are not always up to date. For example, some grammar books say that we should use *whom* rather than *who* after prepositions, but, in fact, except in some situations, *who* is generally used, with a different word order, e.g. 'I've just met the girl who I talked to on Friday' is much more common and accepted than 'I've just met the girl to whom I talked on Friday'.
- Teachers need to keep up to date with what parts of the language are changing and how.
- Grammar rules traditionally describe written language rather than spoken language. For example, repetition, exclamations and **contractions** (two words that are pronounced or written as one, e.g. *don't* from *do not*, *isn't* from *is not*, *won't* from *will not*) are common features of spoken language, but they are not always described in grammar books. Some grammar books are now available which describe spoken language too.
- Very often, speakers of a language can speak and write it well without consciously knowing any grammatical rules or terms.
- Learning some grammatical rules and terms makes language learning easier for some learners. Other learners – e.g. young children – may not find them useful at all.
- Just learning grammatical rules and structures doesn't give learners enough help with learning how to communicate, which is the main purpose of language. So, much language teaching has moved away from teaching only grammar, and now teaches, e.g. functions, language skills and fluency as well as grammar.

*See Units 9–14 for how we learn grammar, Units 15 and 16 for teaching grammatical structures, Units 18, 19 and 20 for planning lessons on grammatical structures and Units 28 and 31 for approaches to and ways of correcting grammar.*

## FOLLOW-UP ACTIVITIES *(See page 171 for answers)*

1 Which part of speech is each of these words? To help you, think of the words in sentences and look at the table on pages 5–6. (Some words are more than one part of speech.)

| | | | | | | |
|---|---|---|---|---|---|---|
| box | during | walk | because | younger | well | wow |
| all | decide | water | we | clever | herself | though |

2 Use prefixes and suffixes to make as many words as you can from these words:
    new        possible        run

3 Find three grammatical structures in your coursebook and complete this table.

| Term | Form | Use |
|------|------|-----|
|      |      |     |
|      |      |     |
|      |      |     |

## REFLECTION

What do you think these learners' comments mean? Do you agree with them? Why?/Why not?
1  Learning grammar doesn't help me to speak English with English-speaking people.
2  Learning grammar rules is really useful, but learning grammatical terms isn't.
3  I didn't need to learn grammar when I learnt my first language.

## DISCOVERY ACTIVITIES

1  Find out which reference materials are available in your school to help you with grammar. Which are most useful? Why?

2  Compare any two of these books on grammar or the grammar information on these two websites. Which do you prefer? Why?
*Practical English Usage* (second edition) by Michael Swan, Oxford University Press 1995
*Discover English* by Rod Bolitho and Brian Tomlinson, Macmillan 1995
*English Grammar In Use* (third edition) by Raymond Murphy, Cambridge University Press 2004
*Uncovering Grammar* by Scott Thornbury, Macmillan 2001
http://www.learnenglish.org.uk
http://www.englishclub.com

3  Use a grammar book or the *TKT Glossary* to find the meaning of these terms:
*active/passive voice, clause, modal verb, phrase, question tag, tense.*

**TKT practice task** *(See page 176 for answers)*

For questions 1-6, match the underlined words in the text below with the parts of speech listed **A-G**. There is one extra option which you do not need to use.

**Parts of speech**

> A conjunction
> B preposition
> C noun
> D adverb
> E pronoun
> F verb
> G adjective

I want you to write a **(1)** <u>list</u> of ten things which **(2)** <u>you</u> like. Do it **(3)** <u>carefully</u>. But don't talk to me or your sister. **(4)** <u>Ask</u> me about any **(5)** <u>difficult</u> words you can't spell. **(6)** <u>When</u> you have finished, you can watch television.

1 ………
2 ………
3 ………
4 ………
5 ………
6 ………

# Unit 2    Lexis

## What is lexis?

**Lexis** is individual words or sets of words, i.e. vocabulary items, that have a specific meaning, for example: *tree*, *get up*, *first of all*.

## Key concepts

What meanings does the word *tree* have?

Vocabulary items have different kinds of meaning. Firstly, there is the meaning that describes the thing or idea behind the vocabulary item, e.g. a tree is a large plant with a wooden trunk, branches and leaves. This meaning is called 'denotation'. Then there is figurative meaning. We speak, for example, of 'the tree of life' or 'a family tree'. This imaginative meaning comes from, but is different from, denotation. There is also the meaning that a vocabulary item has in the **context** (situation) in which it is used, e.g. in the sentence 'We couldn't see the house because of the tall trees in front of it' we understand how tall the trees were partly from knowing the meaning of *tall* and partly from knowing how tall a house is, so the meaning of *tall* in this sentence is partly defined by the context.

The meaning of some vocabulary items is created by adding **prefixes** or **suffixes** to base words (e.g. *unsafe*, *nationality*), or by making **compound words** (two or more words together that have meaning as a set, e.g. *telephone number*, *bookshop*) or by **collocation** (words that often occur together, e.g. *to take a holiday*, *heavy rain*).

To help distinguish the meaning of words from other related words, vocabulary items can be grouped into **synonyms** (words with the same or similar meanings), **antonyms** (words with opposite meanings), and **lexical sets** (groups of words that belong to the same topic area, e.g. members of the family, furniture, types of food). The table below shows some examples.

| Vocabulary items | clear (adjective) | paper (noun) |
|---|---|---|
| Denotations | 1 easy to understand<br>2 not covered or blocked<br>3 having no doubt | 1 material used to write on or wrap things in<br>2 a newspaper<br>3 a document containing information |
| Synonyms | *simple* (for meaning 1)<br>*certain* (for meaning 3) | (none) |
| Antonyms/<br>Opposites | *confusing* (meaning 1),<br>*untidy*, *covered* (meaning 2)<br>*unsure* (meaning 3) | (none) |
| Lexical sets | (none) | *stone*, *plastic*, *cloth*, etc. |

| Vocabulary items | clear *(adjective)* | paper *(noun)* |
|---|---|---|
| Prefixes + base word | *unclear* | (none) |
| Base word + suffixes | *clearly, a clearing* | *paperless* |
| Compounds | *clear-headed* | *paper knife, paper shop, paperback* |
| Collocations | *clear skin, a clear day* | *to put pen to paper* |
| Figurative meanings | *a clear head* | *on paper (e.g. It seemed a good idea on paper)* |

We can see from this table that words sometimes have several denotations. The context in which we are writing or speaking makes it clear which meaning we are using. Words can also change their denotations according to what part of speech they are, e.g. the adjective *clear* vs the verb *to clear*. We can also see that not all words have all the kinds of forms, and that it is not always possible to find synonyms for words, as few words are very similar in meaning.

## Key concepts and the language teaching classroom

- Really knowing a word means knowing all its different kinds of meanings.
- Knowing a word also involves understanding its form, i.e. what part of speech it is, how it works grammatically, and how it is pronounced and spelt.
- Whether we are learning our first or our second language, it takes a long time before we fully know a word. We often recognise a word before we can use it.
- Teachers need to introduce vocabulary items again and again to learners, expanding gradually on their meaning and their forms. This also increases the chances of learners remembering the item.
- We can introduce vocabulary items in reading and listening before we ask learners to use the items.

*See Module 1.2 for factors affecting the learning of vocabulary, Module 1.3 for techniques for the teaching and assessment of vocabulary and Module 2.2 for resources for teaching vocabulary.*

**FOLLOW-UP ACTIVITIES** *(See page 171 for answers)*

1 What does each of these sets of words have in common? Are they synonyms, antonyms, lexical sets, compounds, collocations, words with prefixes or words with suffixes?

  A table, chair, sofa, bed, bookcase, chest of drawers, desk
  B old–young, bright–dark, loud–quiet, fast–slow, first–last, long–short
  C a straight road, a brilliant idea, hard work, no problem, extremely grateful
  D neat–tidy, precisely–exactly, to doubt–to question, nobody–no one
  E microwave, compact disc, toothbrush, paper clip, lampshade, bottle top
  F illness, badly, useless, doubtful, affordable, ability, practical
  G imperfect, rewrite, unable, illiterate, incorrect, ultramodern

2 Put these words in their right place in the first column in the table on the next page:
  compound words      synonyms      antonyms      collocations      denotations
  lexical sets      prefix + base word      base word + suffix

| Term | care *(noun)* | to decide |
|------|------|------|
| A | sensitive attention | to choose one option after thinking about several |
| B | love and attention, worry | to make up your mind |
| C | neglect | to hesitate |
| D | politeness, admiration, respect | to think, to hesitate, to wonder |
| E | (none) | undecided |
| F | careful, careless, carelessness | decided, decidedly |
| G | caretaker | (none) |
| H | great care, take care of | finally decide |

## REFLECTION

Think about these teachers' comments:
1  Beginner learners only need to learn the denotations of words.
2  Learners don't need to learn the names for the different types of meaning.
3  The only way to learn vocabulary is through reading widely.

## DISCOVERY ACTIVITIES

1  Look up three words from your coursebook in an English–English dictionary. What kinds of meanings are given for each word?
2  Look at Chapter 7 'Vocabulary' in *Learning Teaching* by Jim Scrivener, Macmillan 1994. It tells you more about the meaning of words and gives ideas for teaching vocabulary.
3  Look at http://dictionary.cambridge.org and http://www.vocabulary.com. Which is more useful for teaching vocabulary to your learners? Why? Write your answers in your TKT portfolio.
4  Use a dictionary or the *TKT Glossary* to find the meanings of these terms: *affix, homophone, idiom, phrasal verb, register.*

**TKT practice task** *(See page 176 for answers)*

For questions 1-5, match the examples of vocabulary with the categories listed A-F.
There is one extra option which you do not need to use.

Examples of vocabulary
1  impossible, unhappy, disadvantage, rename
2  hard work, a heavy subject, a  great idea
3  wonderful, marvellous, brilliant, great
4  longest, director, wooden, slowly
5  oranges, apples, mangoes, bananas

Categories
A  synonyms
B  collocations
C  compound words
D  lexical set
E  words with suffixes
F  words with prefixes

# Unit 3   Phonology

## What is phonology?

Phonology is the study of the sound features used in a language to communicate meaning. In English these features include phonemes, word stress, sentence stress and intonation.

## Key concepts

Do you know what the signs and symbols in this word mean?

/'stjuːdənt/

A **phoneme** is the smallest unit of sound that has meaning in a language. For example, the *s* in *books* in English shows that something is plural, so the sound /s/ has meaning. Different languages use a different range of sounds and not all of them have meaning in other languages. For example, the distinction between /s/ and /sh/ is an important one in English, where it helps distinguish between words such as *so* and *show*, *sock* and *shock*, *sore* and *shore*. But in Cantonese, you can use either /s/ or /sh/ in words without changing their meaning, i.e. in Cantonese they are not two separate phonemes.

The phonemes of a language can be represented by phonemic symbols, such as /iː/, /aɪ/ and /ɜː/. Each **phonemic symbol** represents only one phoneme, unlike the letters of the alphabet in English where, for example, the letter *a* in written English represents the /æ/ sound in *hat*, the /eɪ/ sound in *made* and the /ə/ sound in *usually*. Phonemic symbols help the reader know exactly what the correct pronunciation is. A **phonemic script** is a set of phonemic symbols which show (in writing) how words are pronounced, e.g. *beautiful* is written /bjuːtɪfl/, *television* is /telɪvɪʒn/ and *yellow* is /jeləʊ/.

Dictionaries use phonemic script to show the pronunciation of words. They usually have a list of all the phonemic symbols at the beginning of the book, together with an example of the sound each symbol represents. The symbols are often grouped into consonants and vowels, and the vowels are sometimes divided into monophthongs (single vowel sounds as in *put* /pʊt/ or *dock* /dɒk/), and **diphthongs** (a combination of two vowel sounds, e.g. the vowel sound in *make* /meɪk/ or in *so* /səʊ/). There are several phonemic scripts and some small differences in the symbols they use. TKT and most learner dictionaries use symbols from the International Phonetic Alphabet (IPA). There is a list of some of these symbols on page 187.

In dictionary entries for words another symbol usually accompanies the phonemic script. This can be ', as in /'bjuːtɪfl/, or _ , e.g. /bjuːtɪfl/ or °, e.g. /bjǔːtɪfl/. These signs are used to show **word stress**. This is the part of the word which we say with greater energy, i.e. with more length and sound on its vowel sound. Compare the **stress** (the pronunciation with greater energy) in the vowel sounds in the stressed syllables and the other syllables in: pen̲cil, chil̲dren, im̲por̲tant. (The stressed syllables are underlined.) We pronounce the other syllables with less energy, especially the **unstressed** or **weak** syllables, whose vowels get shortened or sometimes even disappear, e.g. the vowel sound in the last syllable of *important*, which is pronounced as a schwa /ə/. There are many languages which, like English, give especially strong stress to one syllable in a word, e.g. the Portuguese spoken in Portugal. Other languages give equal length to all the syllables.

In English, stress also influences how sentences and incomplete sentences are pronounced. We say different parts of the sentence with more or less stress, i.e. slower and louder, or quicker and more softly. This is called **sentence stress**. One word in the sentence has **main stress**. This is the word which the speaker thinks is most important to the meaning of the sentence. Other words can have secondary stress. This is not so strong as main stress and falls on words which are not so important to the meaning as the word with main stress. Other words in the sentence are unstressed. For example, in 'She came home <u>late</u> last night' or 'I can't understand a <u>word</u> he says', the words with the main stress are the underlined ones, the words with secondary stress would probably be *came, home, last, night* and *can't, understand, says,* and the unstressed words *she* and *I, a, he.*

Main and secondary stress are usually on content words rather than structural words. Content words are nouns, verbs, adverbs or adjectives, i.e. words that give more information. Structural words are usually prepositions, articles, pronouns or determiners, i.e. words we use to build the grammar of the sentence. For example, in the sentence 'The girl ran to the sea and jumped in quickly' the content words are: *girl, ran, sea, jumped, quickly.* The others are structural words. You can see that normally these would not be stressed. Of course, there are exceptions to this. It is possible to stress any word in a sentence if the speaker thinks it is important. For example, 'The girl ran <u>to</u> the sea and jumped in quickly.' This stresses that she ran towards the sea and not, for example, away from it. Changing the stress of a sentence changes its meaning. Look at these examples:

The <u>girl</u> ran to the sea and jumped in quickly. (i.e. not another person)
The girl ran to the <u>sea</u> and jumped in quickly. (i.e. not to any other place)
The girl ran to the sea and jumped in <u>quickly</u>. (i.e. not in any other way)

Sentence stress is a characteristic of **connected speech**, i.e. spoken language in which all the words join to make a connected stream of sounds. Some other characteristics of connected speech are **contractions** and vowel shortening in unstressed words and syllables, e.g. the schwa sound /ə/ in *potato* /pəteɪtəʊ/ or *London* /lʌndən/. These characteristics help to keep the **rhythm** (pattern of stress) of speech regular. The regular beat falls on the main stress, while the weaker syllables and words are made shorter to keep to the rhythm. Try saying the sentences above and beating out a regular rhythm on your hand as you say them.

**Intonation** is another important part of pronunciation. It is the movement of the level of the voice, i.e. the tune of a sentence or a group of words. We use intonation to express emotions and attitudes, to emphasise or make less important particular things we are saying, and to signal to others the function of what we are saying, e.g. to show we are starting or stopping speaking, or whether we are asking a question or making a statement.

To hear these uses, try saying 'School's just finished' with these meanings: as a statement of fact, with surprise, with happiness, as a question, to emphasise 'just'. You should hear the level of your voice rising and falling in different patterns. For example, when you say the sentence as a statement of fact, your intonation should follow a falling tone as follows: '↘school's just finished'. When you say it as a question, it has a rising tone, as follows: '↗school's just finished', and when you say it with surprise, you will probably say it with a fall-rise tone, as 'ⱽschool's just finished'. Different intonation patterns can show many different meanings, but there is no short and simple way of describing how the patterns relate to meanings. If you want to learn more about intonation, look at the book suggested in the Discovery activities on page 16.

## Key concepts and the language classroom

- Learners of English need to be able to understand a wide variety of accents in English, as English becomes more and more a global language.
- As pronunciation communicates so much of our meaning, producing sounds in a way that can be widely understood is extremely important in language learning. Learners' pronunciation needs to be clear to speakers from many countries.
- A regular focus in lessons on different aspects of pronunciation helps to make learners aware of its importance.
- Teaching materials sometimes include activities or exercises which focus on hearing or producing different sounds in a **minimal pair**, i.e. words distinguished by only one phoneme, e.g. *ship* and *sheep*, *hut* and *hat*, *thing* and *think*, *chip* and *ship*.

*See Modules 2.1 and 2.2 for how to incorporate the teaching of pronunciation into lesson plans and the resources that can be used to do this.*

**FOLLOW-UP ACTIVITIES** *(See page 171 for answers)*

1 Look at the phonemic symbols on page 187. Practise saying each symbol. Learn them, then test yourself or a colleague.
2 How many phonemes are there in each of these words? What are they?
   book      flashcard      number      thirteen      morning
3 Underline the stressed syllable in each of these words:
   twenty      monkey      difficult      forget      remember
4 On which word would you put the main stress in each of these sentences?
   My name is Julia, not Janet.
   Brasilia is in the middle of Brazil, not on the coast.
   The girl was much taller than her older brother. He was really short.
5 Say 'I'm sorry' with these different intonations:
   A a quick apology      B a request for repetition      C with surprise

**REFLECTION**

Think about these comments from teachers. Which do you agree with and why?
1 I don't expect my learners to pronounce the language like a first language speaker.
2 Young children learn good pronunciation naturally. You don't need to teach it to them.
3 Good teachers need to understand phonology.
4 It's not very useful for my learners to learn any of the phonemic symbols.

## DISCOVERY ACTIVITIES

1 Here is an extract from a pronunciation syllabus. Which parts would be relevant for teaching to your learners?

| Lesson | Pronunciation focus |
|---|---|
| 1 | Polite intonation in questions |
| 5 | Intonation in question tags to show agreement |
| Progress check | /i/ and /iː/; being aware of speaker's attitude |
| 7 | Stress and intonation when correcting someone |
| 12 | Word stress in sentences |
| 15 | Stress in compound nouns |

(adapted from *Reward* by Simon Greenall, Macmillan 1995)

2 Find five words you will soon teach your learners. Check their pronunciation in a dictionary. Decide which sounds might be problematic for your learners.

3 Have a look at *Sound Foundations* by Adrian Underhill, Macmillan 1994. It has lots of useful information about different aspects of phonology.

4 Listen to other people's pronunciation and practise your own on this website: http://towerofenglish.com/pronunciation.html

5 Play with the phonemic symbols on this website: http://janmulder.co.uk/Phonmap

6 Use a dictionary and/or the *TKT Glossary* to find the meaning of these terms: *consonant, linking, syllable, voiced/unvoiced sound, vowel.*

. . . . . . . . . . . . . . . . . . . . . . . . . . . . . . . . . . . . . . . . . . . . . . . . . . . . . . . . . . . . . . . . . . . . . . . .

## TKT practice task *(See page 176 for answers)*

For questions 1-5, look at the questions about phonology and the possible answers. Choose the correct answer **A**, **B** or **C**.

1 How many phonemes does the word *heart* have?
   A two                        B three                        C four

2 How is *paper* written in phonemic script?
   A pæper                      B pɪəpə                        C peɪpə

3 Which of the following is true about a stressed syllable?
   A It contains the schwa sound.   B It sounds stronger.      C It is spoken fast.

4 Which of the following is a minimal pair?
   A pin/bin                    B so/sing                      C lot/list

5 Which of the following is a contraction?
   A see you                    B ASAP                         C haven't

. . . . . . . . . . . . . . . . . . . . . . . . . . . . . . . . . . . . . . . . . . . . . . . . . . . . . . . . . . . . . . . . . . . . . . . .

# Unit 4   Functions

## What is a function?

A **function** is a reason why we communicate. Every time we speak or write, we do so for a purpose or function. Here are some examples of functions:

| | | | |
|---|---|---|---|
| apologising | greeting | clarifying | inviting |
| advising | agreeing | disagreeing | refusing |
| thanking | interrupting | expressing obligation | expressing preferences |

Functions are a way of describing language use. We can also describe language grammatically or lexically (through vocabulary). When we describe language through functions we emphasise the use of the language and its meaning for the people who are in the **context** where it is used.

## Key concepts

Look at this table. What do you think an 'exponent' is?

| Context | Exponent (in speech marks) | Function |
|---|---|---|
| A boy wants to go to the cinema with his friend tonight. | The boy says to his friend: 'Let's go to the cinema tonight.' | <u>Suggesting/making a suggestion</u> about going to the cinema |
| A girl meets some people for the first time. She wants to get to know them. | The girl says to the group: 'Hello. My name's Emilia.' | <u>Introducing</u> yourself |
| A customer doesn't understand what a shop assistant has just said. | The customer says to the shop assistant: 'Sorry, what do you mean?' | **<u>Asking for clarification</u>** (i.e. asking someone to explain something) |
| A girl writes a letter to a relative thanking her for a birthday present. | The girl writes 'Thank you so much for my lovely ...' | <u>Thanking</u> someone for a present |

The language we use to express a function is called an **exponent**. The pieces of direct speech in the middle column in the table above are all examples of exponents. In the third column, the functions are underlined. You can see from the table that we use the *ing* forms of verbs (e.g. *suggesting, asking*) to name functions. The words after the function in the third column are not the function. They are the specific topics that the functions refer to in these contexts.

An exponent can express several different functions. It all depends on the context it is used in. For example, think of the exponent 'I'm so tired'. This could be an exponent of the function of describing feelings. But who is saying it? Who is he/she saying it to? Where is he/she saying it? i.e. what is the context in which it is being said? Imagine saying 'I'm so tired' in these two different contexts:

| Context | Function |
|---------|----------|
| A boy talking to his mother while he does his homework | Requesting to stop doing homework |
| A patient talking to her doctor | Describing feelings |

One exponent can express several different functions because its function depends on the context. One function can also be expressed through different exponents.

Here are five different exponents of inviting someone to lunch. How are they different from one another?

Coming for lunch?

Come for lunch with us?

Would you like to come to lunch with us?

Why don't you come for lunch with us?

We would be very pleased if you could join us for lunch.

These exponents express different **levels of formality**, i.e. more or less relaxed ways of saying things. Generally speaking, **formal** (serious and careful) exponents are used in formal situations, **informal** (relaxed) exponents in informal situations and **neutral** (between formal and informal) exponents in neutral situations. It is important to use the level of formality that suits a situation. This is called **appropriacy**. A teacher who greets a class by saying 'I'd like to wish you all a very good morning' is probably using an exponent of the function of greeting that is too formal. A teacher who greets a class by saying 'Hi, guys!' might be using language that is too informal. Both of these could be examples of **inappropriate** use of language. It would probably be **appropriate** for the teacher to say 'Good morning, everyone' or something similar.

## Key concepts and the language teaching classroom

- In language teaching, coursebooks are often organised around functions.
- For example, the map of the book in a coursebook could list functions and language like this:

| Functions | Language |
|-----------|----------|
| Expressing likes | First and third person present simple affirmative: *I like …*, *he/she likes …* |
| Expressing dislikes | First and third person present simple negative: *I don't like …*, *he/she doesn't like …* |

- Functions are often taught in coursebooks together with the grammar of their main exponents. There is an example of this in the map of the book above. You can see that the language in the second column includes 'present simple affirmative', which is a grammatical term, while '*I like …*, *he/she likes …*' are exponents of the function 'Expressing likes'.

- Combining functions and grammar helps to give grammar a meaning for learners and helps them to learn functions with **grammatical structures** that they can then use in other contexts.
- A functional approach to teaching language helps teachers find real-world contexts in which to present and practise grammar, and helps learners to see the real-world uses of the grammar they learn.

*See Units 15 and 16 for teaching activities for functions, Units 18 and 20 for lesson planning and Units 26–27 for classroom functions.*

## FOLLOW-UP ACTIVITIES *(See page 171 for answers)*

1 List at least four different exponents for each of these functions: introducing yourself, suggesting, asking for clarification, thanking.
2 Go through the list of exponents you made in 1 and mark them F (formal), N (neutral) or I (informal).
3 Look at your list of exponents. Which are suitable to teach to a beginners' class?

## REFLECTION

Think about these comments from teachers. Which do you agree with and why?
1 It is easier to teach functions than grammar.
2 Functions contain too much complicated grammar for beginner learners.
3 Learners don't need to learn the names of functions – just some of the exponents.

## DISCOVERY ACTIVITIES

1 Look at the map of your coursebook. Is it organised around functions? What kinds of activities are used in the coursebook units to introduce and practise functions?
2 In your TKT portfolio, list six functions your learners might need to learn to use their English outside the classroom. List the most useful exponents for them, too.
3 To find out more about functions and exponents, look at Chapter 5 of *Threshold 1990* by JA van Ek and JLM Trim, Council of Europe, Cambridge University Press 1998.
4 Here are the names of four common functions: *enquiring, negotiating, predicting, speculating*. Use a dictionary and/or the *TKT Glossary* to find their meanings. Can you think of two exponents for each one?

········································································

**TKT practice task** *(See page 176 for answers)*

For questions 1-6, match the example sentences with the functions listed **A-G**.
There is one extra option which you do not need to use.

| Example sentences | Functions |
|---|---|
| 1 I don't think that's a very good idea. | A describing |
| 2 It's a beautiful place with a big river. | B clarifying |
| 3 He might be able to, I'm not sure. | C comparing |
| 4 What I mean is … | D disagreeing |
| 5 I'd really love to fly to the moon. | E wishing |
| 6 They're much older than their friends. | F suggesting |
| | G speculating |

········································································

# Unit 5    Reading

## What is reading?

Reading is one of the four language **skills**: reading, writing, listening and speaking. It is a **receptive skill**, like listening. This means it involves responding to text, rather than producing it. Very simply we can say that reading involves making sense of text. To do this we need to understand the language of the text at word level, sentence level and whole-text level. We also need to connect the message of the text to our knowledge of the world. Look at this sentence, for example:

The boy was surprised because the girl was much faster at running than he was.

To understand this sentence, we need to understand what the letters are, how the letters join together to make words, what the words mean and the grammar of the words and the sentence. But we also make sense of this sentence by knowing that, generally speaking, girls do not run as fast as boys. Our knowledge of the world helps us understand why the boy was surprised.

## Key concepts

Can you think of reasons why learners may find reading difficult?

A text is usually longer than just a word or a sentence. It often contains a series of sentences, as in a letter or even a postcard. These sentences are connected to one another by grammar and vocabulary and/or knowledge of the world. Reading also involves understanding the connection between sentences. For example:

The boy was surprised because the girl was much faster at running than he was. Then he found out that her mother had won a medal for running at the Olympic Games.

The second sentence gives us a possible reason why the girl was so good at running. But we can only understand that this is a reason if we know that Olympic runners are very good. This means we need to use our knowledge of the world to see the connection between these two sentences (**coherence**). The grammatical links between the sentences (**cohesion**) also help us see the connection between them. For example, in the second example sentence 'he' refers to 'the boy' in the first sentence, and 'her' refers to 'the girl'.

When we read we do not necessarily read everything in a text. What we read depends on why and how we are reading. For example, we may read a travel website to find a single piece of information about prices. But we may read a novel in great detail because we like the story and the characters and want to know as much as we can about them.

These examples show us that we read different text types and we read for different reasons. Some examples of written text types are letters, articles, postcards, stories, information brochures, leaflets and poems. All these kinds of text types are different from one another. They have different lengths, layouts (the ways in which text is placed on the page), topics and kinds of language. Learning to read also involves learning how to handle these different text types.

Our reasons for reading influence how we read, i.e. which reading **subskill** (a skill that is part of a main skill) we use. For example, if we read a text just to find a specific piece or pieces of information in it, we usually use a subskill called **reading for specific information** or **scanning.** When we scan, we don't read the whole text. We hurry over most of it until we find the information we are interested in, e.g. when we look for a number in a telephone directory.

Another reading subskill is **reading for gist** or **skimming**, i.e. reading quickly through a text to get a general idea of what it is about. For example, you skim when you look quickly through a book in a bookshop to decide if you want to buy it, or when you go quickly through a reference book to decide which part will help you write an essay.

A third reading subskill is **reading for detail**. If you read a letter from someone you love who you haven't heard from for a long time, you probably read like this, getting the meaning out of every word.

Another way of reading is **extensive reading**. Extensive reading involves reading long pieces of text, for example a story or an article. As you read, your attention and interest vary – you may read some parts of the text in detail while you may skim through others.

Sometimes, especially in language classrooms, we use texts to examine language. For example, we might ask learners to look for all the words in a text related to a particular topic, or work out the grammar of a particular sentence. The aim of these activities is to make learners more aware of how language is used. These activities are sometimes called **intensive reading**. They are not a reading skill, but a language learning activity.

We can see that reading is a complicated process. It involves understanding letters, words and sentences, understanding the connections between sentences (coherence and cohesion), understanding different text types, making sense of the text through our knowledge of the world and using the appropriate reading subskill. Reading may be a receptive skill but it certainly isn't a passive one!

## Key concepts and the language teaching classroom

- If learners know how to read in their own language, they can transfer their reading skills to reading in English. Sometimes though, they find this difficult, especially when their language level is not high, and they need help to transfer these skills. Teachers need to check which reading subskills their learners are good at, then focus on practising the subskills they are not yet using well, and, if necessary, on teaching them language which will help them do this.

- Giving learners lots of opportunities for extensive reading, in or out of class, helps them to develop their fluency in reading.

- The reading subskills that we need to teach also depend on the age and first language of the learners. Some learners of English, e.g. young children, may not yet know how to read in their own language. They need to learn how letters join to make words and how written words relate to spoken words both in their language and in English. Other learners may not understand the script used in English as their own script is different, e.g. Chinese, Arabic. These learners need to learn the script of English, and maybe also how to read a page from left to right.

- We need to choose the right texts for our learners. Texts should be interesting for learners in order to motivate them. Texts should also be at the right level of difficulty. A text may be difficult because it contains complex language and/or because it is about a topic that learners don't know much about.

- We can make a difficult text easier for learners to read by giving them an easy comprehension task. Similarly, we can make an easier text more difficult by giving a hard comprehension task. This means that the difficulty of a text depends partly on the level of the comprehension task that we give to learners.
- Sometimes we may ask learners to read texts that are specially written or simplified for language learners. At other times they may read articles, brochures, story books, etc. that are what a first language speaker would read. This is called **authentic material**. The language in authentic material is sometimes more varied and richer than the language in simplified texts. Experts believe that learners learn to read best by reading both simplified and authentic materials.
- Different reading comprehension tasks and exercises focus on different reading subskills. Teachers need to recognise which subskill a task focuses on.
- Teachers need to choose comprehension tasks very carefully. They need to be of an appropriate level of difficulty and practise relevant reading subskills.
- The activities in a reading lesson often follow this pattern:
  1 Introductory activities: an introduction to the topic of the text and activities focusing on the language of the text
  2 Main activities: a series of comprehension activities developing different reading subskills
  3 Post-activities: activities which ask learners to talk about how a topic in the text relates to their own lives or give their opinions on parts of the text. These activities also require learners to use some of the language they have met in the text.

*See Unit 16 for activities practising different reading subskills, Module 2.1 for lesson planning and Module 2.2 for resources to help plan lessons.*

## FOLLOW-UP ACTIVITY *(See page 171 for answers)*

Look at this text and activities from a coursebook for intermediate level teenagers and young adults. What does each activity aim to do? Match the activities with the aims in the box. (There is one extra aim.)

| | |
|---|---|
| to relate the text to our world knowledge | to practise skimming |
| to introduce the topic | to practise reading for specific information |

### BEFORE READING

1 Do people eat out a lot in your country?
2 What different kinds of foods are there?

When people think of food in the United States, they think mostly of fast foods like hamburgers and hot dogs. In fact, in U.S. cities like New York and Los Angeles, there are thousands of different kinds of restaurants with foods from all over the world.

So if you like to try different foods, the United States is the place for you. The United States has people from all over the world, and they bring with them typical foods from their countries. You can eat tempura in Japanese restaurants, tacos in Mexican restaurants, paella in Spanish restaurants, pasta in Italian restaurants, and you can also eat America's most popular food, pizza.

Yes, pizza! Pizza is originally from Italy, but today it is an important part of the U.S. menu. There are about 58,000 pizzerias in the United States – that's about 17 percent of all restaurants in the country, and the number is growing.

The United States has eating places for all tastes – and all pockets. You can buy a hot dog on the street and pay one or two dollars. Or you can go to a four-star restaurant and pay $200 for a dinner.

### AFTER READING

A Read the article and fill in the information:

| | |
|---|---|
| 1 Number of different kinds of restaurants in the U.S. | |
| 2 Cost of a meal at a very good restaurant | |
| 3 Cost of a hot dog on the street | |
| 4 Number of pizzerias in the U.S. | |

B Make a typical menu from your country. Include food for breakfast, lunch and dinner.

(adapted from *SuperGoal 2* by Manuel dos Santos, McGraw-Hill 2001)

## REFLECTION

1  What are the easiest and most difficult things for you about reading in English?
2  What helped you most to read English well when you were a learner?

## DISCOVERY ACTIVITIES

1  Look at one text in your coursebook. What text type is it? What reading subskills do its exercises and activities focus on? Is the text interesting and at the right level for the learners? Write your answers in your TKT portfolio.
2  Exchange ideas with colleagues about books or magazines in English that you have enjoyed.
3  Teach a reading lesson. Put your plan and your materials in your TKT portfolio. Include some comments about what was successful/not successful and why. Also comment on how you would improve the lesson next time.
4  Look at these websites:
   http://www.learnenglish.org.uk for reading texts and activities for primary-age learners
   http://kids.mysterynet.com for mystery stories to read and solve
   http://www.thenewspaper.org.uk for newspaper extracts with sports, news and music for teens.
5  Use the *TKT Glossary* to find the meaning of these terms: *deduce meaning from context, prediction, text structure, topic sentence*. Think about how these terms could influence your teaching.

## TKT practice task *(See page 176 for answers)*

For questions 1-5, match the instructions with the ways of reading listed A-F.
There is one extra option which you do not need to use.

### Ways of reading

A  reading for specific information
B  reading for detail
C  reading for gist
D  intensive reading
E  deducing meaning from context
F  extensive reading

### Instructions

1  Find all the words in the story about pets.
2  Read the text. Decide which is the best heading for it.
3  Read the article to find out exactly how the machine works.
4  Finish reading the story at home.
5  Read the poster to find the dates of Annie's, Sam's and Julie's birthdays.

# Unit 6    Writing

## What is writing?

Writing is one of the four language **skills**: reading, writing, listening and speaking. Writing and speaking are **productive skills**. That means they involve producing language rather than receiving it. Very simply, we can say that writing involves communicating a message (something to say) by making signs on a page. To write we need a message and someone to communicate it to. We also need to be able to form letters and words, and to join these together to make words, sentences or a series of sentences that link together to communicate that message.

## Key concepts

What have you written in your language in the past week?

Maybe you have not written anything in the past week! It is true that we do not write very much these days. But possibly you have written a shopping list, a postcard, a birthday card, some emails, your diary, maybe a story. If you are studying, perhaps you have written an essay. All of these are examples of written text types. You can see from this list that text types involve different kinds of writing, e.g. single words only, short sentences or long sentences; use (or not) of note form, addresses or paragraphs, special layouts; different ways of ordering information. When we learn to write, we need to learn how to deal with these different features.

   All written text types have two things in common. Firstly, they are written to communicate a particular message, and secondly, they are written to communicate to somebody. Our message and who we are writing to influence what we write and how we write. For example, if you write a note to yourself to remind yourself to do something, you may write in terrible handwriting, and use note form or single words that other people would not understand. If you write a note for your friend to remind him/her of something, your note will probably be clearer and a bit more polite.

   Writing involves several **subskills**. Some of these are related to **accuracy**, i.e. using the correct forms of language. Writing accurately involves spelling correctly, forming letters correctly, writing legibly, punctuating correctly, using correct layouts, choosing the right vocabulary, using  grammar correctly, joining sentences correctly and using paragraphs correctly.

   But writing isn't just about accuracy. It is also about having a message and communicating it successfully to other people. To do this, we need to have enough ideas, organise them well and express them in an appropriate style.

The table below is from a writing syllabus for primary-school children. The column on the left focuses on accuracy, and the column on the right focuses on communication.

| | |
|---|---|
| • Showing an understanding that letters can be combined to form words, and producing letter shapes, including capital letters, correctly<br>• Using initial capital letters and full stops to indicate sentences<br>• Employing a range of connectives to express sequence (e.g. *next*, *then*) | • Completing simple poems and rhymes with some language support and based on models<br>• Expressing your own experience by supplying labels for your own drawings<br>• Making simple greetings cards and invitations based on models<br>• Responding to greetings and invitations in short notes based on models |

(adapted from *Syllabuses for Primary Schools, English Language, Primary 1–6*, the Education Department, Hong Kong 1997)

Writing also often involves going through a number of stages. When we write outside the classroom we often go through these stages:

- **brainstorming** (thinking of everything we can about the topic)
- making notes
- planning (organising our ideas)
- writing a **draft** (a piece of writing that is not yet finished, and may be changed)
- **editing** (correcting and improving the text)
- producing another draft
- **proof-reading** (checking for mistakes in accuracy) or editing again.

These are the stages of the writing process.

## Key concepts and the language teaching classroom

- The subskills of writing that we teach will vary a lot, depending on the age and needs of our learners. At primary level we may spend a lot of time teaching learners how to form letters and words and write short texts of a few words or sentences, often by copying models. At secondary level we may need to focus more on the skills required to write longer texts such as letters, emails or compositions.
- When we teach writing we need to focus on both accuracy and on building up and communicating a message.
- Sometimes in the classroom learners write by, for example, completing gaps in sentences with the correct word, taking notes for listening comprehension, writing one-word answers to reading comprehension questions. These activities are very useful for teaching grammar, and checking listening and reading, but they do not teach the skills of writing. To teach the writing subskills we need to focus on accuracy in writing, on communicating a message and on the writing process.
- By encouraging learners to use the writing process in the classroom we help them to be creative and to develop their message, i.e. what they want to say.

*See Unit 16 for teaching writing, Unit 20 for planning a lesson and Units 28 and 31 for ways of correcting learners' writing.*

**FOLLOW-UP ACTIVITY** *(See page 172 for answers)*

Here are some suggestions for writing activities. Do they focus on:

    A accuracy    or    B communicating ideas?

1 Reading charts and then writing sentences about them, e.g.:

|  | Tom | Linda |
|---|---|---|
| Swimming | ✓ | ✗ |
| Playing Playstation | ✗ | ✓ |
| Reading | ✓ | ✗ |
| Watching TV | ✗ | ✓ |
| Dancing | ✓ | ✗ |

✓ = likes        ✗ = doesn't like

Example sentence: Tom likes swimming but Linda doesn't.

2 Writing letters, e.g. a letter to a penfriend telling them about yourself.
3 Labelling pictures or objects, e.g. clothes, animals.
4 Completing a story, e.g. the teacher gives the students the beginning, middle or end of a story and asks them to complete the missing part(s).
5 Copying words from a reading book into an exercise book.
6 Writing emails to other students in the school.

**REFLECTION**

1 How did you learn to write English? Was it the best way?
2 What for you are the easiest and most difficult things about writing in English? And for your learners?
3 Which writing subskills do your learners need to focus on most?

## DISCOVERY ACTIVITIES

1 Go back to the list you made of text types you have written this week. Beside each, note your reason for writing and who you wrote to. How did your reason for writing and who you wrote to influence what you wrote? Write your answers in your TKT portfolio.

2 Write an email or a note to a friend. As you write, decide which of these subskills you use: thinking of ideas, ordering ideas, forming correct letters, writing sentences grammatically, linking sentences, checking the accuracy of your writing.

3 Look at one unit in your coursebook and find the activities and exercises on writing. Decide which subskill(s) of writing they aim to develop.

4 Look at these resources to find information, materials and activities on teaching writing:
http://tqjunior.thinkquest.org/5115/s_writing.htm
http://www.hio.ft.hanze.nl/thar/writing.htm
Chapter 8, *How To Teach English* by Jeremy Harmer, Pearson Education Ltd 1998
*Simple Writing Activities* by Jill and Charles Hadfield, Oxford University Press 2000.

5 Use a dictionary or the *TKT Glossary* to find the meaning of these terms: *conclusion, note-taking, paragraph, process writing, summary.*

## TKT practice task *(See page 176 for answers)*

For questions 1-6, match the coursebook instructions with the writing subskills listed **A-G**.
There is one extra option which you do not need to use.

### Writing subskills

A punctuating correctly
B planning
C forming letters
D linking
E using the appropriate layout
F paragraphing
G proof-reading

### Coursebook instructions

1 Put your hand in the air and write d-o-g with your finger.
2 Tick (✓) the correct place in this letter for the address of the receiver and put a cross (✗) in the correct place for the date.
3 This letter has no commas or full stops. Put them in the correct places.
4 Join these pairs of sentences by using the best conjunction from the following: *because, after, while*.
5 Look at this list of ideas for a composition. Number them in the order you would write about them in your composition.
6 Check your work for language mistakes after you have finished writing.

# Unit 7   Listening

## What is listening?

Listening is one of the four language **skills**: reading, writing, listening and speaking. Like reading, listening is a **receptive skill**, as it involves responding to language rather than producing it. Listening involves making sense of the **meaningful** (having meaning) sounds of language. We do this by using **context** and our knowledge of language and the world.

## Key concepts

Listening involves understanding spoken language, which is different from written language.

What differences can you think of between the spoken and written language of English? List some before reading this table.

| Written language in English | Spoken language in English |
|---|---|
| Stays on the page and doesn't disappear. | Disappears as soon as it is spoken. Sometimes it is spoken fast and sometimes slowly, with or without pauses. |
| Uses punctuation and capital letters to show sentences. | Shows sentences and meaningful groups of words through **stress** and **intonation**. |
| Consists of letters, words, sentences and punctuation joined together into text. | Consists of **connected speech**, sentences, incomplete sentences or single words. |
| Has no visual support – except photos or pictures sometimes. | The speaker uses body language to support his/her communication; for example, **gestures** (movements of hands or arms to help people understand us), and **facial expressions** (the looks on our face). This helps the listener to understand what the speaker is saying. |
| Is usually quite well organised: sentences follow one another in logical sequences and are joined to previous or following sentences. | Is not so well organised; e.g. it contains interruptions, hesitations, repetitions and frequent changes of topic. |
| Usually uses quite exact vocabulary and more complex grammar. | Often uses rather general vocabulary and simple grammar. |

To understand spoken language we need to be able to deal with all the characteristics of spoken language listed in the table on page 30. Here is an example of spoken language. You can see that it can be less well organised and less exact than written language:

FATHER:     How's your homework? You know, your history?
SON:        Easy.
FATHER:     You sure?
SON:        It's just … I mean all we need to do is, well, just read some stuff.
FATHER:     But d'you understand it?
SON:        Yeah. Can I go and play with Tom?

To help us understand spoken language we need to use the context the language is spoken in and our knowledge of the world. In this example, our knowledge of relationships between fathers and sons, and of children's attitudes to homework helps us understand, but if we knew the context of the conversation (e.g. the place where it took place, the father's and son's body language, their attitudes to homework), we would understand more.

When we listen, we also need to be able to understand different kinds of spoken text types such as conversations, stories, announcements, songs, instructions, lectures and advertisements. They contain different ways of organising language and different language features, and some consist of just one voice while others consist of more.

We also need to understand different speeds of speech. Some people speak more slowly and with more pauses. Others speak fast and/or with few pauses. This makes them more difficult to understand. We need to understand different accents too (e.g. Scottish or Australian English).

But we do not listen to everything in the same way. How we listen depends on our reason for listening. We might **listen for gist**, **specific information**, **detail**, **attitude** (listening to see what attitude a speaker is expressing), or do **extensive listening**. See page 22 about reading for an explanation of these terms.

We can see that listening involves doing many things: dealing with the characteristics of spoken language; using the context and our knowledge of the world; understanding different text types; understanding different speeds of speech and accents; using different listening **subskills**. Look at this extract from a listening syllabus for lower secondary students of English. It shows many of these different aspects of listening:

- Hearing the differences between common sounds
- Identifying important words in what someone has just said
- Understanding and responding to simple instructions and commands
- Recognising basic differences in information (e.g. commands vs questions)
- Following a simple narrative spoken by the teacher with the help of pictures
- Recognising the sound patterns of simple rhyming words
- Understanding the development of simple stories
- Understanding and responding to simple requests and classroom instructions
- Identifying main ideas

(adapted from *Syllabuses for Secondary Schools, English Language, Secondary 1–5*; the Education Department, Hong Kong 1999)

# Key concepts and the language teaching classroom

- In the classroom, learners can listen to many sources of spoken language, e.g. the teacher, other learners, visitors, cassettes, video, DVDs.
- When we listen to audio cassettes or CDs we can't see the speaker's body language or the context he/she is speaking in. And we can't ask the speaker to repeat or explain. These factors make listening to recordings more difficult than listening to live speakers.
- Some listening texts in coursebooks are **authentic**, i.e. they contain all the features of real spoken language. Other texts are written especially for language learners. Many experts think that learners need to listen to both kinds of text to develop their listening skills.
- Understanding and showing you have understood are not the same thing. For example, maybe you can understand all of a story, but you can't tell the story. So, comprehension activities should be in easier language than the language in the listening text.
- Children learn well from listening to stories that interest them.
- We can develop learners' listening skills by focusing regularly on particular aspects of listening, e.g. problem sounds, features of connected speech, subskills, and, if necessary, on any new language.
- The activities in a listening lesson often follow this pattern:
  1 Introductory activities: an introduction to the topic of the text and activities focusing on the language of the text
  2 Main activities: a series of comprehension activities developing different listening subskills
  3 Post-activities: activities which ask learners to talk about how a topic in the text relates to their own lives or give their opinions on parts of the text. These activities also require learners to use some of the language they have met in the text.

*See Unit 16 for listening activities and Unit 20 for planning lessons.*

**FOLLOW-UP ACTIVITIES** *(See page 172 for answers)*

1 Here is a conversation between two learners of English. Find in it examples of contractions, repetitions, hesitations and interruptions.

| | |
|---|---|
| Yuko: | What would you like your life to be like in 20 years' time? |
| Hiroko: | I'd like it to be … I want to have a family … you know, a husband, three children, my … |
| Yuko: | Would you be happy? |
| Hiroko: | I'd be … I mean, yes. Yeah, sure, sure, of course. What about you? |
| Yuko: | Erm, me, well, erm, er … Maybe I'd like to have a good … you know, to do a really interesting job … with lots of pay, of course! |

(based on a conversation in *English for the Teacher*, Mary Spratt, Cambridge University Press 1994)

2 What do you think is the context of this conversation?
3 Which subskills – gist, detail, specific information or attitude – do the following questions about this conversation focus on?

A What is the conversation about?
B What does Yuko want her life to be like in 20 years' time?
C How many children does Hiroko want?
D Does Hiroko sound happy?

## REFLECTION

Which of the following do you think your learners need most practice in? Why?

Features of connected speech? Which?
Accents? Which?
Speed of speech?
Different text types? Which?
Listening for gist / detail / specific information / attitude?
Extensive listening?

## DISCOVERY ACTIVITIES

1 Find some suitable listening activities in your coursebook. Do them with your learners, and then after the lesson, complete this table in your TKT portfolio:

| What the learners found easy and why | What the learners found difficult and why |
|---|---|
|  |  |

What would you do differently if you taught these activities again?

2 For more information about listening skills and listening activities, read Chapter 10 of *How To Teach English* by Jeremy Harmer, Pearson Education Ltd 1998.

3 Look at these websites for lyrics for songs and ideas for how to use them in class: http://www.eslpartyland.com/teachers/nov/music.htm and http://www.lyrics.com and at this site for all kinds of listening opportunities and activities: http://www.hio.ft.hanze.nl/thar/listen.htm

4 Use the *TKT Glossary* to find the meaning of these terms: *develop skills, infer attitude or mood*.

## TKT practice task *(See page 176 for answers)*

For questions 1-6, match the instructions with the ways of listening listed A-G.
There is one extra option which you do not need to use.

**Instructions**

1 Watch the video to see how the woman looks. How do you think she feels?

2 Listen to each pair of words. Say if they are the same or different.

3 What town does Jim live in? Listen and find out.

4 Listen to the description of the boy and the girl and draw them.

5 Listen and underline the word in the sentence that the speaker says most strongly.

6 Listen to the story and decide what is the best title for it.

**Ways of listening**

A listening for gist
B understanding body language
C listening for individual sounds
D listening for detail
E listening for sentence stress
F extensive listening
G listening for specific information

# Unit 8    Speaking

## What is speaking?

Speaking is a **productive skill**, like writing. It involves using speech to express meanings to other people.

## Key concepts

Tick the things on this list which people often do when they speak.

1  pronounce words
2  answer questions
3  use **intonation**
4  **ask for clarification** and/or explanation
5  correct themselves
6  take part in discussions
7  change the content and/or style of their speech according to how their listener responds
8  greet people
9  plan what they will say
10  smile
11  ask for and give information
12  respond appropriately
13  persuade
14  start speaking when someone else stops
15  tell stories
16  use fully accurate grammar and vocabulary
17  use tenses
18  take part in conversations

We usually do all these things when we speak except 9 and 16. Speaking does not allow us time to do these except in formal speaking such as making speeches. Here is a list of the categories that the other points are examples of:

- grammar and vocabulary (17)
- **functions** (2, 4, 6, 8, 11, 12, 13, 15)
- features of **connected speech** (1, 3)
- **appropriacy** (12)
- body language (10)
- interaction (5, 7, 14, 18).

**Interaction** is two-way communication that involves using language and body language to keep our listener involved in what we are saying and to check that they understand our meaning. Examples of these **interactive strategies** are: making eye contact, using **facial expressions**, asking check questions (e.g. 'Do you understand?'), clarifying your meaning (e.g. 'I mean …', 'What I'm trying to say is …'), confirming understanding (e.g. 'mm', 'right').

We speak with fluency and accuracy. **Fluency** is speaking at a normal speed, without hesitation, repetition or self-correction, and with smooth use of connected speech. **Accuracy** in speaking is the use of correct forms of grammar, vocabulary and pronunciation.

When we speak, we use different aspects of speaking depending on the type of speaking we are involved in. If you go to a shop to buy some sweets and ask the shopkeeper 'How much?', then leave after he/she replies, you don't use many of them. If you go to the bank to ask the bank manager to lend you $500,000, you will probably need to use many more. If you eat a meal with all your relatives, you will also use many in conversation with them. As you can see, speaking is a complex activity.

## Key concepts and the language teaching classroom

- We can develop learners' speaking skills by focusing regularly on particular aspects of speaking, e.g. fluency, pronunciation, grammatical accuracy, body language.
- In many classes learners do **controlled practice** activities (activities in which they can use only language that has just been taught). These are a very limited kind of speaking because they just focus on accuracy in speaking and not on communication, interaction or fluency. Controlled practice activities can provide useful, if limited, preparation for speaking.
- Tasks and less controlled practice activities give more opportunity than controlled activities for learners to practise communication, interaction and fluency.
- Sometimes learners speak more willingly in class when they have a reason for communicating, e.g. to solve a problem or to give other classmates some information they need.
- Because speaking is such a complex skill, learners in the classroom may need a lot of help to prepare for speaking, e.g. practice of necessary vocabulary, time to organise their ideas and what they want to say, practice in pronouncing new words and expressions, practice in carrying out a task, before they speak freely.
- Learners, especially beginners and children, may need time to take in and process all the new language they hear before they produce it in speaking.
- The activities in a speaking lesson often follow this pattern:
  1 **Lead-in**: an introduction to the topic of the lesson plus, sometimes, activities focusing on the new language
  2 Practice activities or tasks in which learners have opportunities to use the new language
  3 Post-task activities: activities in which learners discuss the topic freely and/or ask the teacher questions about the language used.

*See Units 15 and 16 for speaking activities, Unit 20 for planning lessons and Units 28 and 31 for correcting speaking.*

FOLLOW-UP ACTIVITY (See page 172 for answers)

The titles of some materials on teaching speaking are numbered 1–10 below. Match the titles with the aspects of speaking (A–E) that they focus on. Some titles focus on more than one aspect.

A accuracy    B connected speech    C appropriacy    D fluency    E functions

1 Intonation in *wh-* questions (*what, when, where, why, how*)
2 Language for asking for polite clarification
3 Informal language for greeting
4 Language for agreeing and disagreeing
5 Using past tenses in stories
6 Distinguishing minimal pairs of sounds
7 Disagreeing politely
8 Using intonation to show doubt
9 Taking part in discussions
10 Telling stories

REFLECTION

1 How did your teachers teach you the speaking skill in English? Did you have enough practice in all aspects of speaking?
2 Which aspects of speaking English do you find most easy and difficult now?
3 Do you teach speaking in the same way you were taught it? Why?/Why not?

DISCOVERY ACTIVITIES

1 Look at a unit in your coursebook. Which aspects(s) of speaking does it focus on most?
2 Listen to a short conversation or story on the cassette from your coursebook. Which of the six categories on page 34 does it contain examples of?
3 Record yourself telling a story in English. Then listen to yourself. What are the weak and strong points in your use of connected speech? Practise, and then record yourself again. Have you improved? Put your analysis in your TKT portfolio.
4 Look at this website to find speaking activities your learners can do: http://towerofenglish.com
5 These books have lots of speaking activities. Are there any you can do with your classes?
*Elementary Communication Games* by Jill Hadfield, Pearson Education Ltd 1992
*Simple Speaking Activities* by Jill and Charles Hadfield, Oxford University Press 1999

**TKT practice task** *(See page 176 for answers)*

For questions 1-7, match the activities with the teaching focuses listed **A**, **B** or **C**.

Teaching focuses

**A** appropriacy
**B** fluency
**C** connected speech

Activities

1 Identifying particular phonemes in conversations on audio cassette
2 Practice in speaking at a natural speed
3 Practice in greeting people informally
4 Identifying main stress in short dialogues on audio cassette
5 Practice in speaking without hesitating
6 Practice in using exponents of formal invitations
7 Practice in using intonation to show surprise

# Part 2 | Background to language learning

## Unit 9  Motivation

### ▪ What is motivation?

**Motivation** is the thoughts and feelings we have which make us want to do something, continue to want to do it and turn our wishes into action, i.e. motivation influences:

- why people decide to do something
- how long they want to do it for
- how hard they are prepared to work to achieve it.

Motivation is very important in language learning. It helps make learning successful.

### ▪ Key concepts

Why were/are you motivated to learn English? List your reasons.

Many factors influence our motivation to learn a language. These factors include:

- the usefulness to us of knowing the language well, e.g. for finding jobs, getting on to courses of study, getting good marks from the teacher
- our interest in the **target language culture** (the culture of the language we are learning)
- feeling good about learning the language: success, **self-confidence** (feeling that we can do things successfully), **learner autonomy/independence** (feeling responsible for and in control of our own learning)
- encouragement and support from others, e.g. teacher, parents, classmates, school, society
- our interest in the learning process: the interest and relevance to us of the course content, classroom activities, the teacher's personality, teaching methods.

Learners may have strong motivation in one of these areas and little in another, or their motivation may be quite balanced. Different learners will also be motivated in different ways from one another, and motivation can change. Learners may, for example, be quite uninterested in learning a particular language, then meet a teacher who they like so much that they begin to love learning the language. Motivation can change with age, too, with some factors becoming more or less important as learners get older. We can see that motivation needs to be both created and continued.

### ▪ Key concepts and the language teaching classroom

Here are some suggestions from two experts on motivation about how teachers can encourage greater motivation in their learners.

---

1 Set a personal example with your own behaviour (i.e. be motivated as a teacher yourself).

2 Create a relaxed atmosphere in the classroom (i.e. try to prevent anxiety in yourself or the learners).

3 Present tasks in an interesting way which makes the tasks seem achievable to the learners.

4 Develop a good relationship with the learners.

5 Increase the learners' self-confidence about language learning (i.e. help learners feel they can be good at learning the language).

6 Make the language classes interesting.

7 Promote learner autonomy.

8 **Personalise** the learning process (i.e. make the course feel relevant to the learners' lives).

9 Increase the learners' awareness of their **goals** (i.e. what they want to achieve).

10 Familiarise learners with the target language culture.

---

(adapted from 'Ten commandments for motivating language learners: results of an empirical study' by Z. Dörnyei and K. Csizér, *Language Teaching Research*, Hodder Arnold 1998)

*See Units 29–32 for how motivation influences classroom management.*

## FOLLOW-UP ACTIVITY *(See page 172 for answers)*

Here are some classroom activities. Which of the above ten suggestions do you think they aim at? (Some may aim at more than one.)

A Giving learners a story about skateboarding because you know many of them like skateboarding

B Encouraging learners to meet some first language speakers of English

C Giving learners a test which is quite easy for most of them

D Asking learners which of four tapes they would like to listen to in the next lesson

E Giving learners reading texts about working in an English-speaking country

F Teaching with enthusiasm and interest

G Presenting the language to learners in small bits which they are able to learn easily

H Talking to a learner after class about the problems in their last homework, and how they can make better progress

I Encouraging and praising learners, even weak ones

J Making sure your lessons are varied and well-paced

K Your learners love doing crosswords – you find another one for them to do

## REFLECTION

1 What is learning English like? Here are some answers from teenage learners. Do they seem motivated?

Learning English is like:

a) a fish getting water – easy, helpful, necessary.

b) bread – plenty of resources and opportunities, but none of them are very good.

c) rice – you need it every day. But you get bored with it because you have it all the time.

d) learning the piano – I have learnt it for many years and am still not very good at it.

2 Do you agree with the ten suggestions above for motivating learners?

## DISCOVERY ACTIVITIES

1 Look at these resources. Are any of them suitable for motivating your learners?
http://www.eslpartyland.com/teachers/nov/music.htm
http://www.learnenglish.org.uk
http://www.english-zone.com
*Communication Games* (Beginners', Elementary, Intermediate) by Jill Hadfield, Pearson Education Ltd 1999, 1992 and 1992
*English Grammar In Use* (third edition) by Raymond Murphy, Cambridge University Press 2004

2 Exchange ideas with another teacher about ways of increasing your learners' motivation, or ask another teacher if you could watch part/all of a lesson of theirs to see how they encourage motivation.

3 Think about a lesson or part of a lesson that you taught which really interested your learners. Why were they so interested? How could you encourage that interest again in a future lesson? Put your ideas in your TKT portfolio. Share them with a colleague.

## TKT practice task *(See page 176 for answers)*

For questions 1-7, match the teaching recommendations with the influences on motivation listed A-H.
There is one extra option which you do not need to use.

### Influences on motivation

A learner autonomy
B interest in the lesson
C interest in the target culture
D the usefulness of learning the language
E personalisation
F goal-setting
G support from others
H self-confidence

### Teaching recommendations

1 Where possible, ask learners to choose what activities they want to do.
2 Encourage parents to motivate their children to learn English.
3 Remind learners how important English is for getting jobs.
4 Choose activities and materials that are motivating.
5 Bring to the classroom any materials (e.g. brochures, photos, souvenirs) you have collected on your trips to English-speaking countries.
6 Praise learners frequently but honestly.
7 Give learners opportunities to use English to talk about their own lives.

# Unit 10    Exposure and focus on form

## What are exposure and focus on form?

Across the centuries people have studied how foreign languages are learnt. Many experts now believe that one way we learn a foreign language is by **exposure** to it, i.e. by hearing and/or reading it all around us and without studying it. They say we then **pick it up** automatically, i.e. learn it without realising. This is the main way that children learn their first language.

Experts also say that to learn a foreign language, particularly as adults, exposure to language is not enough. We also need to **focus** our attention **on the form** of the foreign language, i.e. on how it is pronounced or written, on how its grammar is formed and used, and on the form and meaning of vocabulary. They say we need to use language to interact and communicate, too.

## Key concepts

Have you learnt English more successfully from formal study or just by picking it up?

Research has identified three main ways in which we learn a foreign language. Firstly, experts talk of us **acquiring** language. This means the same as picking it up. They say that to really learn a foreign language we need exposure to lots of examples of it, and that we learn from the language in our surroundings. We need to hear and read lots of language which is rich in variety, interesting to us and just difficult enough for us, i.e. just beyond our level, but not too difficult. **Acquisition** takes place over a period of time, i.e. not instantly, and we listen to and read items of language for a long time before we begin to use them (a **silent period**).

Secondly, to learn language we need to use it in **interaction** with other people. We need to use language to express ourselves and make our meanings clear to other people, and to understand them. The person we are talking to will show us, directly or indirectly, if they have understood us or not. If they have not, we need to try again, using other language, until we manage to communicate successfully.

Thirdly, research shows that foreign language learners also need to focus on form. This means that they need to pay attention to language, e.g. by identifying, working with and practising the language they need to communicate.

Nowadays, experts generally agree that we do not learn a foreign language best through learning grammar and translating (the **grammar–translation method**). Nor do we learn by constantly practising until we form habits (the behaviourist or structuralist approach) or just by communicating (the **communicative approach**). We learn by picking up language, interacting and communicating and focusing on form. But the research still continues, and we do not yet fully understand how foreign languages are learnt.

## ■ Key concepts and the language teaching classroom

- To acquire language, learners should hear and read a wide variety of language at the right level for them. They need exposure to language both inside and outside the classroom.
- Learners need time to acquire language. They may need a silent period before they can produce new language and we cannot expect them to learn things immediately. Learning language is a gradual process.
- Learners need to use language in the classroom to interact with classmates or the teacher. This gives them the opportunity to experiment with language and find out how successful their communication is.
- Learners need opportunities to focus on forms of language they have read or listened to in texts or used in tasks. The teacher can help them to notice certain points about language, think about their use and practise them.
- But we need to remember that some learners may like to learn and/or are used to learning in particular ways. Teachers always need to match their teaching to the characteristics and needs of the learner.

*See Units 12, 13 and 14 for the different characteristics and needs of learners and Unit 16 for ways of focusing on and practising language, and for examples of communicative tasks.*

**FOLLOW-UP ACTIVITY** *(See page 172 for answers)*

Put these classroom activities into the correct column in the table according to which way of learning they encourage most. (Some may go into more than one column.)

| Acquisition | Interaction | Focus on form |
|---|---|---|
|  |  |  |

1  The learners listen to the teacher read a story.
2  The learners do an oral pairwork task about choosing a birthday present for someone.
3  The learners underline examples of the past simple tense in a text.
4  A learner asks the teacher what the English word for … is.
5  The teacher corrects a learner's pronunciation of a word.
6  The learners categorise words in a list into different lexical sets.
7  A group of learners research a topic and then present their results to the rest of the class.
8  A role-play in which one learner gives another advice about a problem on a cue card.
9  While the learners have a class discussion, the teacher listens and tells them new words when they don't know them but need to use them.
10  The learners write sentences each containing an example of the new structure they have just been taught.

## REFLECTION

1 Which method of learning English would you prefer: communicative, form-focused, grammar–translation, or a combination of these? Why?

2 What method(s) do your learners seem to prefer? Why? Do you agree with their preferences?

## DISCOVERY ACTIVITIES

1 Look at http://www.eltforum.com for articles discussing how languages are learnt.

2 Identify one learner who seems to prefer a communicative style of learning and another who prefers learning language forms. Interview them (in their own language if necessary) about how they prefer to learn language and why they prefer this way. *Or* observe them in class and see how they each react to different kinds of activities. Write down your observations and put them in your TKT portfolio.

**TKT practice task** *(See page 176 for answers)*

For questions 1-5, choose the correct option **A**, **B** or **C** to complete each statement about learning language.

1 The group of learners who generally benefit most from picking up language is:
   A children under the age of five.
   B people over the age of 20.
   C teenagers aged 15–19.

2 Being exposed to the right level of language helps learners
   A check their own progress.
   B increase their interaction.
   C acquire more language.

3 A silent period is a time when learners
   A do written work.
   B study the language.
   C process the language.

4 Acquiring language involves
   A studying the grammar carefully.
   B listening just to language-focused exercises.
   C learning language just by hearing or reading it.

5 When we focus on the form of language we
   A talk with classmates.
   B pay attention to accuracy and use.
   C listen to videos and audio cassettes.

# Unit 11    The role of error

## ◾ What is the role of error?

This unit focuses on mistakes learners make when they speak or write English. Mistakes are often divided into **errors** and **slips**. **Errors** happen when learners try to say something that is beyond their current level of language processing. Usually, learners cannot correct errors themselves because they don't understand what is wrong. Errors play a necessary and important part in language learning, as we will see below. **Slips** are the result of tiredness, worry or other temporary emotions or circumstances. These kinds of mistakes can be corrected by learners once they realise they have made them.

## ◾ Key concepts

There are two main reasons why learners make errors. Can you think what they are?

There are two main reasons why second language learners make errors. The first reason is influence from the learner's first language (**L1**) on the second language. This is called **interference** or transfer. Learners may use sound patterns, lexis or grammatical structures from their own language in English.

The second reason why learners make errors is because they are unconsciously working out and organising language, but this process is not yet complete. This kind of error is called a **developmental error**. Learners of whatever mother tongue make these kinds of errors, which are often similar to those made by a young first language speaker as part of their normal language development. For example, very young first language speakers of English often make mistakes with verb forms, saying things such as 'I goed' instead of 'I went'. Errors such as this one, in which learners wrongly apply a rule for one item of the language to another item, are known as **overgeneralisation**. Once children develop, these errors disappear, and as a second language learner's language ability increases, these kinds of errors also disappear.

Errors are part of learners' **interlanguage**, i.e. the learners' own version of the second language which they speak as they learn. Learners unconsciously process, i.e. analyse and reorganise their interlanguage, so it is not fixed. It develops and progresses as they learn more. Experts think that interlanguage is an essential and unavoidable stage in language learning. In other words, interlanguage and errors are necessary to language learning.

When children learn their mother tongue they seem to speak their own form of it for a while, to make progress on some language items, then to go backwards, and to make mistakes for a time before these mistakes finally disappear, usually without obvious correction.

Errors are a natural part of learning. They usually show that learners are learning and that their internal mental processes are working on and experimenting with language. We go through stages of learning new language, and each new piece of language we learn helps us learn other pieces of language that we already know more fully – like pieces of a jigsaw puzzle which only make full sense when they are all in place.

Developmental errors and errors of interference can disappear by themselves, without correction, as the learner learns more language. In fact, correction may only help learners if they are ready for it, i.e. they are at the right stage in their individual learning process. But experts believe that learners can be helped to develop their interlanguage. There are three main ways of doing this. Firstly, learners need exposure to lots of interesting language at the right level; secondly they need to use language with other people; and thirdly they need to focus their attention on the forms of language. (See Unit 10 for more about these three ways.)

Sometimes errors do not disappear, but get 'fossilised'. Fossilised errors are errors which a learner does not stop making and which last for a long time, even for ever, in his/her foreign language use. They often happen when learners, particularly adults, are able to communicate as much as they need to in the foreign language and so have no communicative reason to improve their language. These fossilised errors may be the result of lack of exposure to the **L2** (second language) and/or of a learner's lack of motivation to improve their level of accuracy.

## Key concepts and the language teaching classroom

- We need to think hard about whether, when and how to correct learners.
- We mustn't expect instant learning. Learning is gradual, and errors will occur.
- We need to think about what kind of mistake the learner is making – a slip or an error.
- If the mistake is a slip, the learner can probably correct him/herself, maybe with a little prompting from the teacher or another learner.
- Sometimes, particularly in fluency activities, it is better not to pay attention to learners' errors (i.e. **ignore** them) so that the learners have an opportunity to develop their confidence and their fluency, and to experiment with language.
- Some errors may be more important to correct than others. Those which prevent communication are more important than those which do not, e.g. missing the final *s* off the third person singular of a present simple tense verb doesn't prevent communication. But using the present simple tense instead of the past simple tense can sometimes prevent communication.
- We need to think about what is best for the learning of each learner. Different learners within the same class may need to be corrected or not, depending on their stage of learning, learning style and level of confidence. Different learners may also need to be corrected in different ways.
- Ways of helping learners get beyond their errors are:
  – to expose them to lots of language that is just beyond their level through reading or listening
  – to give them opportunities to focus on the form of language
  – to provide them with time in class to use language to communicate and interact and see if they can do so successfully.
- A good time to correct learners or to provide them with new language is when they realise they have made a mistake or need some new language. We should encourage learners to ask us for this help.
- Errors are useful not only to the learner but also to the teacher. They can help the teacher see how well learners have learnt something and what kind of help they may need.

*See Unit 28 for categories of mistakes, Unit 31 for how to correct learners and Unit 32 for how to give feedback.*

**FOLLOW-UP ACTIVITY** *(See page 172 for answers)*

Here is a conversation between two elementary-level learners of English. They are doing a fluency activity in which they talk about the hobbies they would like to start. The woman is Japanese and the man is Spanish.

Read it and notice how the learners are trying their best to communicate, and giving one another help in communicating.

N.B. The words in *italics* in brackets (...) are spoken by the other speaker at the same time as the main speaker.

| | |
|---|---|
| Woman: | Oh if, if you can (*mm*) um, what hobbies you would like to start? |
| Man: | Yes, I like er so much the, to play the piano (*ah, play piano*), it is one of my, my dreams (*dream, ah your dream, ah, yes*) because when I listen (*yes*) the piano music (*yes*) I, I imagine, I imagine a lot of things (*ah*), beautiful things (*yes, ah I see*) a um I like so much the, the piano (*play piano*) play the piano (*yes*). And you? |
| Woman: | Um, yes, er, I want to, I want to learn (*to learn*) to dance (*to dance*) um flamenco (*flamenco*) yes (*Spanish flamenco*) yes flamenco. When I finish my school I maybe, I'll go to Spain (*mm*) to learn (*to learn flamenco*) yeah, yes flamenco (*mm*) yes and then … would, would you like to (*laughter*) … |
| Man: | And I play an instruments too. |
| Woman: | No I can't, I can't, I can't play anything, any instrument (*yeah*) even piano (*mm*). So how about you? (*yeah*) Could you, can you play – |
| Man: | No, I play nowaday the guitar, nothing more (*guitar, oh it's good*) yeah, the Spanish guitar (*yes, oh it's lovely*) the sound is lovely. |
| Woman: | Yes, yes, one day (*yeah*) please, please play the guitar for me. |
| Man: | Of course (*yeah*), of course. |

(from *English for the Teacher* by Mary Spratt, Cambridge University Press 1994)

**REFLECTION**

Do you agree with these teachers' and learners' comments? Why?/Why not?
1 I like my teacher to correct all my mistakes.
2 If I don't correct my students, they will continue to make the same mistakes and these will become bad habits.
3 It's impossible in class for a teacher to know why a student is making a mistake.
4 It's difficult to use different correction techniques with different students.

## DISCOVERY ACTIVITIES

1 Look at a piece of writing from one of your learners and underline all the mistakes. What might be the cause of the mistakes? Are they all worth correcting? Discuss this with another teacher if you can. Write your analysis in your TKT portfolio.
2 To learn more about why learners make mistakes and how we can correct them, read Chapter 7 of *The Practice of English Language Teaching* (third edition) by Jeremy Harmer, Pearson Education Ltd 2001.
3 Use a dictionary or the *TKT Glossary* to find the meaning of *cognitive*.

**TKT practice task** *(See page 176 for answers)*

For questions 1-6, match the statements with the types of mistakes listed **A-C**.

Types of mistakes

**A** a slip
**B** interference
**C** a developmental error

Statements
1 All beginners confuse the tenses in English.
2 The learner was extremely tired. This made her forget lots of grammar.
3 The learner was able to correct his own mistake.
4 The learner's pronunciation was full of sounds from his own language.
5 Nearly all the learners, of whatever mother tongue, made mistakes with the word order in English present simple tense question forms.
6 He was very angry so he kept making mistakes.
7 The learner kept using vocabulary based on her own language.

# Unit 12    Differences between L1 and L2 learning

## ■ What are the differences between L1 and L2 learning?

When we learn our first language (**L1**) we are likely to learn it in different ways and in different contexts from when we learn a second language (**L2**). We are also likely to be a different age.

## ■ Key concepts

What differences can you think of between L1 and L2 learning? Think about the learners' age, ways of learning and **context** that they are learning in.

|  | L1 learning | L2 learning (in the classroom) |
|---|---|---|
| Age | • Baby to young child. (L1 learning lasts into adolescence for some kinds of language and language skills, e.g. academic writing.) | • Usually at primary school and/or secondary school. It can also start or continue in adulthood. |
| Ways of learning | • By **exposure** to and **picking up** language.<br>• By wanting and needing to communicate, i.e. with strong **motivation**.<br>• Through **interaction** with family and friends.<br>• By talking about things present in the child's surroundings.<br>• By listening to and taking in language for many months before using it (**silent period**).<br>• By playing and experimenting with new language. | • Sometimes through exposure but often by being taught specific language.<br>• With strong, little or no motivation.<br>• Through interaction with a teacher and sometimes with classmates.<br>• Often by talking about life outside the classroom.<br>• Often by needing to produce language soon after it has been taught.<br>• Often by using language in controlled practice activities. |
| Context | • The child hears the language around him/her all the time.<br>• Family and friends talk to and interact with the child a lot.<br>• The child has lots of opportunities to experiment with language. | • The learner is not exposed to the L2 very much – often no more than about three hours per week.<br>• Teachers usually simplify their language. |

|  | L1 learning | L2 learning (in the classroom) |
|---|---|---|
| Context | • Caretakers* often **praise** (tell the child he/she has done well) and encourage the child's use of language.<br>• Caretakers simplify their speech to the child.<br>• Caretakers rarely correct the form and accuracy of what the child says in an obvious way. | • Teachers vary in the amount they praise or encourage learners.<br>• The learner receives little individual attention from the teacher.<br>• Teachers generally correct learners a lot. |

* Caretakers are people who look after a child. Often they are parents. But they may also be brothers or sisters, other members of the family, etc.

It is not always easy to describe L2 learning in the classroom because it happens in different ways in different classrooms. The description in the table above may not be true of all classrooms.

Of course, L2 learning sometimes takes place outside the classroom when children or adults pick up language. In this situation, L2 learning is more similar to L1 learning, except that the learner often does not get as much exposure to the language as the L1 learner and may not be so motivated to learn.

Another big difference between L1 and L2 learning is that L1 learning is nearly always fully successful, while L2 learning varies a lot in how successful it is.

## Key concepts and the language teaching classroom

- Foreign language learners need to be exposed to a rich variety of language, use it to communicate and interact, and have opportunities to **focus on form**. This helps to make the circumstances of L2 learning more similar to those in L1 learning and allows L2 learners (who are usually older than L1 learners) to use their different abilities to process language.
- Motivation is very important in language learning, so we should do all we can to motivate learners (see Unit 9).
- Learners are different from one another (in learning style, age, personality, etc. – see Units 13 and 14) so we should try to **personalise** our teaching to match their learning needs and preferences. We can do this by varying our teaching style, approaches, materials, topics, etc.
- Learners may find a silent period useful, but some learners, especially adults, may not.
- We should encourage learners to use English as much as possible in their out-of-class time. This increases their exposure to it. They could, for example, listen to radio programmes or songs, read books or magazines, look at websites, make English-speaking friends, talk to tourists, write to English-speaking penfriends, etc.
- We should try to simplify our language to a level that learners can learn from, and avoid correcting them too much. They need to build up their fluency, motivation and confidence, and have opportunities to pick up and experiment with language.
- In the classroom we should try to praise learners and give them as much individual attention as we can.

## FOLLOW-UP ACTIVITIES *(See page 172 for answers)*

1 Look at these two pictures. What differences that influence language learning can you imagine between the two language learning situations? Think of at least five.

2 Here are two learners. Which way would you suggest for them to improve their English, A, B or C?

Fatima, aged ten, is Moroccan and speaks Arabic. She lives in the capital, Rabat, with her family. She is just starting to learn English at school.

A Go and study in an English-speaking country.
B Use English when playing with a friend.
C Do lots of extra homework.

Ricardo, aged 40, is Brazilian. He lives in the capital, Brasilia, with his wife and four children. He has never learnt English before but needs it for his new job as a taxi driver.

A Chat to as many foreign tourists as possible.
B Study English grammar by himself.
C Go to conversation classes.

## REFLECTION

1 How did your age, and the ways and context in which you learnt English influence your success at learning?
2 What would help your learners to learn English better?

## DISCOVERY ACTIVITIES

1 Look at a unit in your coursebook. Find some activities which encourage interaction, exposure to language or motivation.
2 Look at this website:
http://www.eltforum.com
It often has interesting articles about how we learn languages and how to teach different age groups of learners. It also has teacher chat rooms.
3 Use the *TKT Glossary* to find the meaning of these terms: *activity-based learning, deductive learning, inductive learning*.

## TKT practice task *(See page 176 for answers)*

For questions 1-9, match the features of learning with the learners listed **A**, **B** or **C**.

### Learners

A  L1 learner
B  L2 beginner classroom learner
C  both the L1 learner and the L2 beginner classroom learner

### The features of learning

1  The learner is very often surrounded by language that is interesting to him/her.
2  The learner picks up language from the rich language that surrounds him/her all day.
3  The learner learns with family and friends.
4  The learner often hears language that focuses on just one learning point.
5  The learner uses the language in controlled practice activities.
6  The learner often makes mistakes.
7  The learner usually receives lots of individual encouragement.
8  The learner often stays silent for a long time before finally speaking.
9  The learner needs time to process new language.

# Unit 13   Learner characteristics

## ◼ What are learner characteristics?

Learner characteristics are differences between learners which influence their attitude to learning a language and how they learn it. These differences influence how they respond to different teaching styles and approaches in the classroom, and how successful they are at learning a language. The differences include a learner's motivation, personality, language level, learning style, learning strategies, age and past language learning experience.

## ◼ Key concepts

Can you think of how the ways in which you like to learn, how you have learnt in the past and your age might influence how you prefer to learn a language?

*Learning styles*

**Learning styles** are the ways in which a learner naturally prefers to take in, process and remember information and skills. Our learning style influences how we like to learn and how we learn best. Experts have suggested several different ways of classifying learning styles. They relate to the physical sense we prefer to use to learn, our way of interacting with other people and our style of thinking. Here are some commonly mentioned learning styles:

| visual | the learner learns best through seeing |
|---|---|
| **auditory** | the learner learns best through hearing |
| **kinaesthetic** | the learner learns best through using the body |
| group | the learner learns best through working with others |
| individual | the learner learns best through working alone |
| reflective | the learner learns best when given time to consider choices |
| impulsive | the learner learns best when able to respond immediately |

You can see from these descriptions how learners with different learning styles learn in different ways, and need to be taught in different ways. We must remember though, that learners may not fall exactly into any one category of learning style, that different cultures may use some learning styles more than others and that learners may change or develop their learning styles.

*Learning strategies*

**Learning strategies** are the ways chosen and used by learners to learn language. They include ways to help ourselves identify what we need to learn, process new language and work with other people to learn. Using the right strategy at the right time can help us learn the language better, and help to make us more independent or **autonomous** learners. Some examples of learning strategies are:

- repeating new words in your head until you remember them
- experimenting/taking risks by using just learnt language in conversations
- guessing the meaning of unknown words
- asking the teacher or others to say what they think about your use of language
- deciding to use the foreign language as much as possible by talking to tourists
- recording yourself speaking, then judging and correcting your pronunciation
- asking a speaker to repeat what they have said
- deciding what area of vocabulary you need to learn and then learning it
- thinking about how to remember all the new words you meet in each lesson and then deciding to write each new one on a separate card
- **paraphrasing** (using other language to say what you want to say).

Different learners use different strategies. Experts think that the strategies that learners use most successfully depend on their personality and learning style. This means there are no best strategies. But research shows that using strategies definitely makes learning more successful and that learners can be trained to use strategies.

*Maturity*

Maturity involves becoming grown up physically, mentally and emotionally. Children, teenagers and adults have different learning characteristics and therefore learn in different ways. Here are some of the main differences in maturity that influence language learning:

| Children | Teenagers | Adults |
|---|---|---|
| Need to move | Starting to keep still for longer periods but still need to move | Able to keep still for longer periods |
| Can concentrate for shorter periods | Concentration developing | Can concentrate for longer periods |
| Learn through experience | Beginning to learn in abstract ways, i.e. through thinking, as well as experiencing | Learn in more abstract ways |
| Are not very able to control and plan their own behaviour | Beginning to control and plan their own behaviour | Usually able to control and plan their own behaviour |
| Are not afraid of making mistakes or taking risks | May worry about what others think of them | Not so willing to make mistakes or take risks |
| Are not aware of themselves and/or their actions | Sometimes uncomfortably aware of themselves and/or their actions | Aware of themselves and/or their actions |
| Pay attention to meaning in language | Pay attention to meaning and increasingly to form | Pay attention to form and meaning in language |
| Have limited experience of life | Beginning to increase their experience of life | Have experience of life |

Of course, every learner is different, so someone may not fit exactly into these descriptions. They are generalisations that show likely, but not fixed, characteristics. But from looking at these differences we can see that each age group needs to be taught in different ways.

*Past language learning experience*

Teenage and adult learners may have learnt English before. They may be used to learning in a particular way and have definite ideas about how to learn best. For example, an adult may have learnt English at school through learning lots of grammar and may have been successful in learning this way. If he then finds himself in a class where the teaching is done just through asking learners to use language for communication, he may not like learning in this new way. Another adult may have learnt by using translation at school and then come to a class in which translation is never used. She may or may not like this change. Teachers of adults (and sometimes teachers of teenagers) need to be aware of how their learners have learnt previously and how they want to learn now. The learners may welcome a change in method but they may want to learn in the same way as they learnt before. Teachers may need to discuss and explain their methods to learners who are unhappy with new methods. They may also need to change their teaching to make the learner more comfortable and confident in their learning.

## Key concepts and the language teaching classroom

- Learners are not all the same. They do not all learn in the same way.
- Some learner characteristics, such as past language learning experience and learning strategies, are more relevant to teaching teenagers and adults than to teaching children.
- We can find out what our learners' characteristics are by asking them, observing them, giving them questionnaires, asking at the end of a lesson whether they liked the activities done in class and why, and in what different ways they might like to work.
- Learner characteristics may not be fixed. We must not limit a learner by thinking they can only learn in a particular way.
- We can train learners to become aware of and use different learning strategies.
- It is not possible for the teacher of a big class to meet the learner characteristics of each learner all the time. Across a number of lessons teachers can try to vary how they teach so that they can match the learner characteristics of a range of learners.

**FOLLOW-UP ACTIVITIES** (See pages 172–3 for answers)

1 Look at these descriptions of three learners. How might their learner characteristics influence how they like to learn and how successful they are at learning English?

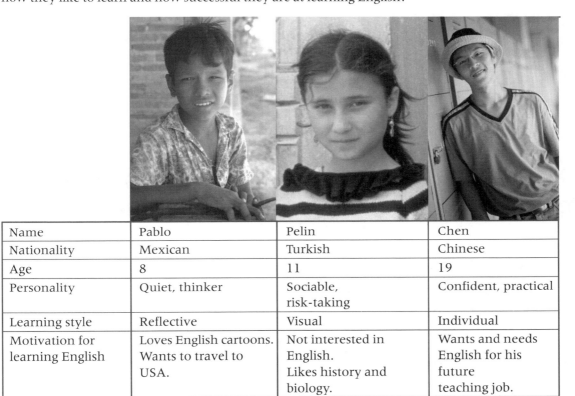

| Name | Pablo | Pelin | Chen |
|------|-------|-------|------|
| Nationality | Mexican | Turkish | Chinese |
| Age | 8 | 11 | 19 |
| Personality | Quiet, thinker | Sociable, risk-taking | Confident, practical |
| Learning style | Reflective | Visual | Individual |
| Motivation for learning English | Loves English cartoons. Wants to travel to USA. | Not interested in English. Likes history and biology. | Wants and needs English for his future teaching job. |
| Past experience of learning English | None | Four years at primary school learning songs, listening to stories and playing games. | Fourteen years at school. Learnt lots of grammar. |

2 Look at these classroom activities and at the list of learning styles on page 52. Match the activities with the learning styles they are most suitable for.

A reading a text slowly and carefully before answering questions
B playing a team running game
C writing in groups
D discussing how to improve pronunciation after a speaking task
E listening to stories
F writing new vocabulary in an exercise book
G writing a composition on your own
H a speaking fluency activity

Do you think all these activities are suitable for both adults' and young children's classes?

## REFLECTION

1  What is your learning style?
2  What strategies do you use/have you used to help you learn English?
3  What is your past experience of learning English?

## DISCOVERY ACTIVITIES

1  Observe two of your learners next week and work out which learning style(s) they have. Write a description of their learning style(s) and put it in your TKT portfolio.
2  Look at the questionnaires on learning styles on these websites:
   http://www.ncsu.edu/felder-public/ILSpage.html
   http://www.vark-learn.com/english/page.asp?p=questionnaire
   Use them to discover your learning style. Also, are they – or any part of them – suitable for giving to your learners?
3  Use the *TKT Glossary* to find the meaning of these terms: *attention span, learner training, self-access centre.*

**TKT practice task** *(See page 176 for answers)*

For questions 1-7, match what the learner does with the learning strategies listed A-D.
You need to use some options more than once.

### Learning strategies

A  taking risks
B  getting organised
C  judging your own performance
D  working with others

### What the learner does

1  The learner collects new vocabulary on cards and then sorts the cards into topics.
2  The learner paraphrases to say something beyond his level of language.
3  The learner guesses an unknown word from the context.
4  The learner compares a recent composition with an old one, to see if she has made progress.
5  The learner decides to buy a dictionary for use at home.
6  The learner solves a problem with his classmates.
7  The learner records herself reading aloud and then listens to the recording to see if her pronunciation is good.

# Unit 14   Learner needs

## What are learner needs?

When a learner learns a foreign language he or she has various kinds of needs which influence his/her learning. They are personal needs, learning needs and future professional needs. Meeting these learner needs is part of being a good teacher.

## Key concepts

Can you think of any learner needs that your learners have?

The different kinds of learner needs are shown in this table:

| LEARNER NEEDS | |
| --- | --- |
| *Kind of needs* | *Where the needs come from* |
| Personal needs | age<br>gender<br>cultural background<br>interests<br>educational background<br>**motivation** |
| Learning needs | **learning styles**<br>past language learning experience<br>learning gap (i.e. gap between the present level and the target<br>    level of language proficiency and knowledge of the target culture)<br>learning **goals** and expectations for the course<br>**learner autonomy**<br>availability of time |
| (Future) professional needs | language requirements for employment, training or education |

(based on 'What do teachers really want from coursebooks?' by Hitomi Masuhara in *Materials Development in Language Teaching*, ed. Brian Tomlinson, Cambridge University Press 1998)

We can see from the table that different learners have different needs. This means they need to be taught in different ways and learn different things in the English classroom.

# Key concepts and the language teaching classroom

Adults or older teenagers with specific professional, general or academic goals for learning English need courses that meet their needs. Here, for example, is a range of different kinds of professional, general and academic English courses. Notice the differences there are between them.

1  A four-week intensive course on exam strategies for taking a university entrance exam.
2  A series of one-to-one lessons over eight weeks on business presentation skills.
3  A six-month course for future tourists focusing on speaking and listening for social and daily survival English.
4  A year-long course on writing academic essays and reading academic books and articles.
5  A short summer course in the UK for teenagers, involving lots of sports, trips to tourist sites and chatting with English teenagers.
6  A once-a-week course for a small group of accountants held in the learners' company, a large accountancy firm, on teaching English for accountants.
7  A four-week online course on writing business letters in English.

You can see that to meet the future needs of learners these courses vary in length, frequency, class size, language skill focused on, type of English, teaching methods and activities.

Learners at primary or secondary school may not yet have professional or academic needs, but they do have personal and learning needs in English. Meeting these needs presents the teacher with various choices for the classroom. These are shown in the table below.

| Learner needs | How the teacher can meet learner needs |
|---|---|
| Personal needs | Choosing suitable:<br>• materials<br>• topics<br>• **pace** (speed) of lessons<br>• activities<br>• approach to teaching (e.g. activity-based, topic-based)<br>• treatment of individual learners<br>• **skills**<br>• **interaction patterns** (e.g. group, pair or individual work)<br>• types of **feedback** (comments on learning) |
| Learning needs | Choosing suitable:<br>• materials and topics<br>• activities<br>• interaction patterns<br>• approach to teaching<br>• language and skills<br>• level of language and skills<br>• **learning strategies**<br>• workload |

*See Unit 9 for motivation in teaching and learning, Unit 13 for the effects of learner characteristics on teaching and learning and Unit 20 for lesson planning.*

## FOLLOW-UP ACTIVITIES *(See page 173 for answers)*

1  Look at these descriptions of two learners. Make notes on their possible learning needs in the English classroom.

*Tatyana*

*Gul*

- Age 6, female
- Russian father, French mother, lives in Paris
- Loves activities and sport and being with other people
- Started learning English two months ago
- Learns English happily because she enjoys her class and likes her teacher

- Age 30, male
- Indian, lives in India – rarely meets people from other countries
- Needs to improve his English for his new job as a hotel manager
- Very interested in computer programming
- Started learning English at age 7 in primary school and has excellent grammar, weak speaking skills, good writing skills, little knowledge of hotel English
- Wants to learn quickly and to a high level
- Very busy; little time for lessons

2  Here are some teacher choices. Which of the learner needs on page 57 do they aim to meet? (Some choices may aim at more than one need.)

A  Choosing to read the learners a fairy story
B  Focusing on the specific pronunciation problems of the class
C  Deciding that three learners should work alone while the rest do group work
D  Choosing to focus on the language of oral presentations with a class of adult professionals
E  Focusing on developing learners' ability to read for detail in preparation for an exam
F  Deciding to put the learners in groups for the whole term and only do group work

G  Teaching learners to use a dictionary and the spell checker on the computer
H  Deciding to ask the learners why they are learning English and what they hope to achieve with it
I  Deciding to only praise and never criticise a particular learner
J  Choosing to take the class to the computer laboratory rather than the classroom to write a composition

## REFLECTION

Think about these comments from teachers. Which do you agree with and why?

1 I cannot think about my students' needs when I have 40 students in a class. All I can do is teach the materials in my coursebook.
2 When I find a topic and activities that my students are interested in, they seem to wake up and really enjoy my lessons.
3 Satisfying my students' needs gives me satisfaction as a teacher.

## DISCOVERY ACTIVITIES

1 Choose one of your learners, and over the next week or two try to identify his or her learner needs. It might be useful to interview the learner to help you do this. When you have a clear idea of the learner's needs, think about how you could teach this learner best. Write a description of the learner's needs and your teaching ideas for your TKT portfolio.
2 Ask a colleague if you can observe one of her/his classes. Or video one of your own classes, then watch it. As you observe, try to notice all the different needs the learners show during the lesson.

**TKT practice task** *(See page 176 for answers)*

For questions 1-7, match the descriptions of the learners with the causes of their needs listed **A-H**. There is one extra option which you do not need to use.

### Causes of needs

A lack of motivation
B learner autonomy
C past learning experience
D learning style
E learning gap
F learning goals
G availability of time
H professional

### Descriptions of learners

1 The learner really needs to learn English well to succeed in her job.
2 The learner learns best through working alone.
3 The learner has an extremely busy job and can only learn English in the evenings.
4 The learner has serious pronunciation problems which prevent him passing an oral exam.
5 The learner is used to learning lots of grammar.
6 The learner finds the English classes boring.
7 The learner needs to learn how to learn English by herself, as she can't afford to go to classes.

# Part 3 | Background to language teaching

## Unit 15    Presentation techniques and introductory activities

## ▪ What are presentation techniques and introductory activities?

Presentation techniques are ways used by the teacher to **present** (introduce to learners for the first time) new language such as vocabulary, grammatical structures and pronunciation. Introductory activities are those used by a teacher to introduce a lesson or teaching topic.

## ▪ Key concepts

Look at the **presentation** stages (the areas that are shaded) in these descriptions of two lessons for elementary-level secondary-school students. How are the stages different?

| Presentation, Practice and Production (PPP) lesson | Task-based Learning (TBL) lesson |
|---|---|
| Aim: students learn the difference between countable and uncountable nouns, and when to use *a* and *some* with them. | Aim: students choose food and drinks for a birthday party. |
| Procedure: | Procedure: |
| 1  Ask students what food and drink they like at birthday parties. | 1  Hold a discussion with the students about when their birthdays are, what presents they would like, what good birthday parties they have been to and what they like to eat and drink at birthday parties. |
| 2  Stick on the board magazine pictures of different party foods. (They should be a mixture of countable and uncountable nouns e.g. *ice cream, sandwiches, cola, fruit, bananas, chicken legs, cake, a box of sweets*.) | 2  Put students into small groups and give them a worksheet with the pictures, names and prices of lots of party food and drink on it. |
| 3  Ask students the names of the food items, write the names on the board under each picture and then do a quick choral drill on the pronunciation of these words. | 3  Tell the students to do this task: choose the food and drink they would like for a birthday party for ten friends keeping within a price limit e.g. $10. |
| 4  Say to students: 'I'm having a birthday party this weekend. I'd like a box of sweets and a cake for my party. And I'd like some ice cream, some cola and some fruit. I'd also like some sandwiches, some bananas and some chicken legs.' | 4  The students do the task while the teacher goes round the class listening and answering any questions. |
|  | 5  Each group tells the other groups what decisions they have made. |

| Presentation, Practice and Production (PPP) lesson | Task-based Learning (TBL) lesson |
|---|---|
| 5 Say 'I'd like a box of sweets', 'I'd like a cake', I'd like some ice cream', etc., and ask students to repeat each sentence chorally. | 6 The students ask the teacher questions about any language they needed for the task and/or the teacher tells the students about any language she noticed they didn't know while they were doing the task, e.g. the pronunciation of some food words, the grammar of uncountable and countable nouns. |
| 6 Point out to the students that you can count some nouns but you can't count others. These are called countable and uncountable nouns. You use *a* with singular countable nouns and *some* with uncountable nouns or plural countable nouns. | |
| 7 Ask the students some concept questions, e.g. 'Which of the food items on the board are countable/uncountable/singular/plural?' | 7 Students do a written exercise on the new language. |
| 8 Students do a written gap-fill exercise, filling the gaps with *a* or *some*. | |
| 9 Students work in pairs with a worksheet of pictures of food and drink items. One student tells the other what they'd like for their party, e.g. 'I'd like some/a ...', while the other student takes notes. Then they swap roles. | |

The introductory stage of a lesson helps students to settle into the lesson and focus on its content. There are two kinds of introductory activities: **warmers** and **lead-ins**. Warmers are often used to raise students' energy levels or to make them feel comfortable. They are not always connected to the topic of the lesson, for example, they could be a quiz, game or pairwork activity. Lead-ins focus on the topic or new language of the lesson. They can also focus and motivate students and make a link between the topic of the lesson and the students' own lives (**personalisation**). For example, if in one lesson students are going to read a text about the Internet, rather than giving them the text immediately, we could do one or more lead-in activities such as discussing with students how often they use the Internet, what they use it for, what their favourite websites are, etc. Or if in another lesson they are going to listen to a conversation about favourite television programmes, the lead-in activities might be making a list of their favourite television programmes and discussing them with a partner. These activities will probably lead on to teaching relevant vocabulary for the texts and comprehension tasks to follow.

If you look back at the PPP and TBL lessons on page 61 you will see that they too include introductory activities. Step 1 in the PPP lesson provides a lead-in to the topic, and steps 2 and 3 a lead-in for language needed for the lesson's main aim. In the TBL lesson, steps 1 and 2 are lead-ins.

## Key concepts and the language teaching classroom

The two lessons on pages 61–2 show two common and different approaches to presenting new language items. The lesson on the left is an example of a PPP lesson, the lesson on the right an example of a TBL lesson. There are many differences between them.

In the **Presentation, Practice and Production (PPP)** lesson:

- The lesson has a language aim.
- The teacher first **contextualises** the new language, i.e. puts it into a situation which shows what it means. (Step 1)
- The teacher then makes sure that the students remember previously studied language needed to practise the new language by **eliciting** it, i.e. asking students to say the language rather than giving it to them, and by doing **a choral drill** (getting the students to repeat as a whole class what he/she says). (Steps 2–3)
- The teacher next presents the new language and the students just listen. (Step 4)
- The students then say sentences including the new language in a very **controlled** or **restricted practice** activity, i.e. one in which they can use only the new language and without making mistakes. (Step 5)
- The teacher tells students about the grammatical use of the new language. (Step 6)
- The teacher asks the students **concept questions**, i.e. questions that check their understanding of the use or meaning of the new language. (Step 7)
- The students then carry out another controlled practice activity. (Step 8)
- The students do **less controlled** or **freer practice** (i.e. where they can use their own ideas) using the new language. (Step 9)

You can see that in a PPP lesson the teacher:

1 presents new language in a **context**
2 gets students to practise it in controlled practice activities
3 asks the students to use the new language in less controlled activities, in a communicative way.

In the **Task-based Learning (TBL)** lesson:

- The aim of the lesson is for the students to complete a **task** (an activity in which students try to achieve something real, and have to communicate to do so).
- The teacher starts by holding a discussion on the topic of the lesson. (Step 1)
- The teacher then gives the students tasks to do. (Steps 2, 3, 4, 5)
- Then the teacher and students discuss any new or problematic language they needed for the task. (Step 6)
- Lastly, the students do an exercise on the new language. (Step 7)

You can see that in a TBL lesson the teacher:

1 gives students tasks to do
2 presents new language after students have needed to use it, and only presents language that he/she or the students have identified as needed.

A PPP approach to presenting new language gives students an opportunity to practise language in a safe learning environment where it is difficult to make mistakes. It can therefore be quite a confidence-building approach for students. But it makes students learn language items they may not be interested in or ready to learn and gives them few opportunities to really use the language for communication. The TBL approach, on the other hand, allows students to find new language when they want to, and to use language experimentally and creatively for real communication. In this way it puts second language learners in a situation which is quite similar to the one in which children learn their first language. Some learners may find this approach to language learning exciting and challenging. Others may wish for more guidance and structure to help them.

PPP and TBL are not the only ways of presenting new language. It is also possible, for example, to present new language to learners after they have met it in a reading or listening text which is first used for comprehension. Another possibility is to hold a discussion on a topic and introduce new language in the context of the discussion; another one is to give learners a task that requires them to use new language, then after the task, present the new language to them and then give them another task to practise the new language (**Test-teach-test**).

Presenting new language involves making various choices:

- When to present the new language? Before (as in PPP) or after (as in TBL) learners try to use the new language?
- What and how many language items to present (new grammatical structures, new vocabulary, new lexical phrases, new functional exponents, new topics)? In PPP the teacher makes this choice; in TBL the teacher and/or the learners make the choice.
- What context to present the new language in? In both TBL and PPP new language items are presented in a **meaningful** context, i.e. one that shows the meaning of the new language, and is **personalised**.
- What aids to use to help create the context, e.g. pictures, video, cassette, a worksheet?
- How to show the meaning or use of the new language, e.g. explanation, translation, presenting through a situation?
- What aspects of the new language to present, i.e. one, some or all of the following: meaning/use, pronunciation, grammar, spelling?

Introductory activities involve the teacher in selecting interesting and relevant warmers and lead-ins. The warmers make the students feel comfortable and ready for the lesson, and the lead-ins introduce the topic of the lesson and main language points needed by the learners to complete the main tasks of the lesson. You may not always need to do warmers as learners may arrive at a lesson ready to learn.

The ways you present new language or introduce lessons will depend on your learners – their level, interests, age, what language they already know, weaknesses and strengths in English and **learning styles**. They will also depend on the resources available to you in your school and the approach to presentation used in your coursebook.

*See Unit 16 for types of activities and tasks, Unit 18 for selecting language for presentation and planning a lesson, Units 23–25 for resources and materials useful for presentation and Unit 26 for classroom functions often used by the teacher to present new language.*

## FOLLOW-UP ACTIVITY *(See page 173 for answers)*

Which of these are presentation activities?

1  The teacher says two new functional exponents and asks the learners to repeat them.
2  The learners read a newspaper article and do a comprehension task on it.
3  The learners ask the teacher how to say … in English and the teacher tells them.
4  The teacher points out to learners that in the task many of them mispronounced the word *station*. She asks them to repeat it after her.

5 The learners have a discussion.
6 The learners translate a short poem into their own language.
7 The teacher uses a picture story to create a context for introducing *he* and *she*.

## REFLECTION

Think about these comments from teachers. Which do you agree with and why?
1 TBL is close to the way we learn new language in our first language.
2 Learners prefer a PPP to a TBL approach.
3 I always present new language in the same way as I was taught at school.

## DISCOVERY ACTIVITIES

1 Look at a unit in your coursebook that presents new language. Does it use PPP, TBL or another approach?
2 Present some new language to a class using PPP and to another using TBL. Analyse the strong and weak points of each. Put your analysis in your TKT portfolio.
3 For more ideas on presenting new language, read Chapter 12 of *Learning Teaching* by Jim Scrivener (2nd edition, Macmillan 2005).
4 Find or create some warmers. Do one with a class and in your TKT portfolio, note the effect it had on the learners and the lesson.
5 Use the *TKT Glossary* to find the meaning of these terms: *definition, icebreaker, illustrate meaning, lexical approach, situational presentation.*

**TKT practice task** *(See page 176 for answers)*

For questions 1-6, match the parts of a presentation stage with the names listed **A-G**.
There is one extra option which you do not need to use.

| Parts of a presentation stage | Names |
|---|---|
| 1 *went, came, chose, swam, ate, thought, ran* | A concept question |
| 2 The teacher tells the learners about a wonderful holiday she went on last summer. | B aids in presentation |
| 3 Photos of last summer's holiday. | C context for presentation |
| 4 The teacher asks: 'When am I talking about, the past, the present or the future?' | D freer practice activity |
| 5 The teacher drills pronunciation of new words. | E language selected for presentation |
| 6 The teacher says: 'We use the past tense to talk about actions in the past that have completely finished.' | F controlled practice activity |
| | G explanation of use |

# Unit 16  Practice activities and tasks for language and skills development

## ■ What are practice activities and tasks for language and skills development?

These are activities and tasks designed to give learners opportunities to practise and extend their use of language, such as new vocabulary, functional **exponents** or **grammatical structures**, or of the **subskills** of reading, listening, speaking or writing. There are many different kinds of activities and tasks with different names and different uses.

## ■ Key concepts

Here are two writing activities.  Can you find three teaching differences between them?

*Activity 1*

> Complete these sentences about yourself with *can* or *can't*.
> 1  I .......... swim.
> 2  I .......... speak Mandarin.
> 3  I .......... play the guitar.
> 4  I .......... use a computer.
> 5  I .......... run very fast.

*Activity 2*

> Write an invitation inviting your friends to your birthday party.
> • Invite them.
> • Tell them:
>   the date
>   the time
>   the address of the party.

We can see that both these activities give learners an opportunity to use language, but in different ways.

*Activity 1*

*Activity 2*

• is a **controlled/restricted practice** activity because learners can only use certain items of language
• focuses on accurate use of language
• is a gap-fill exercise.

• is a **less controlled/freer practice** activity because the language the learners will use is not carefully limited or controlled
• focuses on communicating a message
• is a **task**.

The same kinds of differences can also be seen in other activities for speaking, writing and learning new language. **Drills** (guided repetitions), copying words or sentences, jazz chants, dictation and reading aloud are other examples of controlled practice activities. In freer activities the teacher or the materials do not limit the language that learners use. Examples of these are:

discussions; solving problems through exchanging ideas; sharing or comparing ideas, information or experiences; writing emails, stories, letters, invitations or compositions.

Here are six more activities. What skill/subskill/language do they focus on? What is the name of the type of activity?

1  Read the story. Then answer these questions:
   a  How old is the girl?
   b  Where does she live?
   c  What is her friend's name?

2  A  Listen to the tape and choose the best answer:
      The children's school is:
      a  near their house
      b  near the shops
      c  opposite the post office
   B  Now listen again. Are these sentences true or false?
      a  The school is new.
      b  The classroom is big.
      c  The library has many books.

3  Look at these pictures and then read the story. Put the pictures in the correct order. Write the correct number (1–6) under each picture.

4  Listen to the tape, and in pairs fill in this form:
   Girl's name: ..........................................
   Girl's address: ......................................
   Name of girl's friend: ...........................

5  Work in pairs. Each of you should use one of these role cards.

   A  Your friend has a problem. Give him/her the best advice you can.

   B  You have a problem. You want to go to university, but you find studying very difficult. Ask your friend for advice.

6  Get into groups of four. Find out which food your friends like and dislike most. Ask:
   Which food do you like most?
   Which food do you dislike most?

Here are the answers to the questions above:

| Activity | Skill/subskill/language | Type of activity |
|---|---|---|
| 1 | **Reading for specific information** | Wh- questions (questions beginning with question words: e.g. *which/what/how/when/why*) for comprehension |
| 2 | **Listening for specific information** | A **Multiple-choice questions** (an activity in which you choose the best answer from three or more possible answers) B **True/False questions** (an activity in which you decide whether statements are correct or incorrect) |
| 3 | **Reading for detail** | Ordering |
| 4 | **Listening for specific information** | Form filling |
| 5 | **Fluency** in speaking / freer practice of new language | **Role-play** (an activity in which you imagine that you are someone else in a specific situation) |
| 6 | **Accuracy** in speaking / controlled practice of new language | **Survey** (finding out the opinions of a group on one topic) |

We can see that activities can differ in several ways: the skill or subskill they focus on; what type they are and what **interaction patterns** they use. The kinds of skills or the language they focus on and the interaction patterns they use are not fixed. So, for example, multiple-choice questions could be used for reading, listening or grammar activities and can be done individually, in pairs or in groups. Similarly, form-filling could be used for reading, listening or grammar practice, and done individually, in pairs or in groups.

Activities 5 and 6 both involve learners talking to one another to exchange information they don't know. This means they are talking in order to communicate, not just to practise language. This kind of activity in which learners exchange information that only one of them has is called an **information gap** or a **communicative activity**.

An activity may focus on accuracy or communication depending on how it is introduced by the teacher or the materials. For example, the survey above is focused on accuracy because it limits the language that learners use to ask and answer two specific questions. If the instructions for the activity were 'Find out about your friends' likes and dislikes in food', this would not restrict learners' choice of language and the activity would focus on communication.

## Key concepts and the language teaching classroom

- When selecting activities for practising language or the skills of speaking or writing, we need to decide whether to do a controlled practice or a freer practice activity, an activity that focuses on accuracy or on communication.
- When choosing activities for developing skills, we need to decide which skill or subskill to focus on.
- Lessons usually consist of a series of linked activities. There are several different ways of linking activities in lessons. These are just some of them:
  1 **PPP**: Presentation → controlled practice activities → freer practice activities
  2 **TBL**: Discussion → tasks → presentation → focus on form
  3 Skills-based lessons: **Warmer** and **lead-in** → comprehension tasks → post-task activities
  Example 1: A listening skills lesson
  Lead-in: discussing the topic of the listening and learning any important new vocabulary → Comprehension tasks: listening to the recorded conversation and answering multiple-choice gist questions about it → listening to the conversation again and completing a form with specific information → Post-task activities: brief discussion of the topic of the conversation.
  You can see that the comprehension activities (for listening or reading) start with focusing on more general levels of comprehension before moving on to subskills that require paying more detailed or specific attention to the text.
  Example 2: A topic-based lesson which develops several skills
  Lead-in: speaking about the topic and doing related language work → Tasks: listening to a recording about the topic → reading a text about the topic → Post-task activities: discussing the topic and/or focus on the language of the topic → writing a composition about the topic.

See Units 18 and 20 for planning activities for lessons and Unit 26 for language useful to the teacher for carrying out activities.

## FOLLOW-UP ACTIVITIES *(See page 173 for answers)*

1  What do these activities aim to develop? Put them into the correct column.

| Communication | Accuracy |
|---|---|
|  |  |

A  choral drilling of pronunciation
B  role-play
C  dictation
D  discussions
E  gap-fill exercises
F  story writing
G  copying words
H  repeating new words
I  describing pictures
J  learning conversations by heart
K  problem solving

2  Which skill(s) could these activities be used to develop?

A  story completion
B  form-filling
C  information gap
D  true/false questions
E  role-play

## REFLECTION

Think about these learners' comments:
1  I don't like doing lots of different activities – it's confusing.
2  I like doing a mixture of activities with some focusing on accuracy and some on fluency. That really helps me learn.

## DISCOVERY ACTIVITIES

1  Look through two pages of your coursebook. Can you name all the different kinds of activities it contains? What is the purpose of each activity?
2  Look at http://www.learnenglish.org.uk to see lots of different activities for developing skills and language.
3  Look back over this unit and find a type of activity that you have never taught before. Try it with one of your classes. Did it work well? Was it successful? Write up your thoughts in your TKT portfolio.
4  Use the *TKT Glossary* to find the meaning of these terms: *chant, jumbled pictures, labelling, prioritising, project work.*

## TKT practice task *(See page 176 for answers)*

For questions 1-7, match the descriptions with the teaching activities listed **A-H**.
There is one extra option which you do not need to use.

### Teaching activities

A  problem solving
B  a role-play
C  labelling
D  choral drilling
E  form filling
F  a game
G  a survey
H  project work

### Descriptions

1  The teacher says a word and asks all the learners to repeat it together.
2  The teacher puts learners in pairs and asks one of them to act as a lost tourist asking the way, and the other as a local person giving directions.
3  The learners use maps to work out the best way to get from X to Y.
4  The learners listen to a tape and complete a timetable.
5  The learners ask all their classmates their opinion about something and then note it down.
6  The learners go to the local museum, the library and the Internet to find out about dinosaurs. They then make an exhibition of wall posters about them.
7  The learners choose names of objects from a list and write the names under pictures of the objects.

# Unit 17   Assessment types and tasks

## What are assessment types and tasks?

**Assessment** means judging learners' performance by collecting information about it. We **assess** learners for different reasons, using different kinds of tests to do so. Assessment tasks are the methods we use for assessing learners. We can assess learners informally or formally. **Informal assessment** is when we observe learners to see how well they are doing something and then give them comments on their performance. **Formal assessment** is when we assess learners through tests or exams and give their work a mark or a grade.

## Key concepts

List all the reasons you can think of for assessing learners.

There are several reasons why we might want to assess learners:

1  At the beginning of a course we might give them a test to find out what they know and don't know. This is called a **diagnostic test**. The information from the assessment helps us decide what to teach and which learners need help in which areas of language.
2  When learners go to a language school or evening classes, the school may want to know what level the learners are, so they give them a test. This is called a **placement test**. We use the information from a placement test to decide what level of class the learners should go into.
3  After we have finished teaching a part of a course we may want to find out how well learners have learnt it. This is called **formative assessment**. If we use a test for this purpose it is called a **progress test**. We use the information from formative assessment to decide if we need to continue teaching this area or not, and to give learners **feedback** on their strengths and difficulties in learning in this area.
4  At the end of a term or course, we may assess learners to see how well they have learnt the contents of the whole course. This kind of assessment is called **achievement** or summative testing. Learners usually receive a score or mark from this kind of testing and sometimes feedback on their performance.
5  Sometimes learners take tests to see how good they are at a language. This kind of test is called a **proficiency test**. The contents of the test are not based on a course or syllabus that the learner has followed.

Learners can also assess themselves (**self-assessment**) or one another (**peer assessment**). They usually do this informally with checklists to guide them. The reason for using both of these kinds of assessment is to help learners to understand their language use and performance better, and so become more **autonomous**.

There are many different assessment tasks, e.g. gap-fill, **multiple-choice questions**, **true/false questions**, ordering, correcting mistakes, taking part in interviews, conversations or **role-plays**, writing letters or compositions, dictation. There are some important differences between these tasks:

- Some tasks are like tasks we use outside the classroom to communicate, e.g. a conversation, an interview, a letter, reading a leaflet for prices. These tasks test communication skills.
- Some tasks, e.g. gap-fill, test the **accuracy** of language use. We do not use them to communicate, and they do not test communication skills.
- Some tasks, such as gap-fill or choosing between pairs of sounds, just test one thing, e.g. learners' knowledge of the past tense, or their ability to distinguish between sounds.
- Some tasks, such as a composition or a conversation, test many things together. A composition, for example, tests spelling, handwriting, punctuation, grammar, vocabulary, organisation of ideas and fluency of writing. A conversation can test pronunciation, **appropriacy**, accuracy, **fluency** and **interaction**.
- The answers to some kinds of assessment tasks are easy to mark because they are either right or wrong, e.g. in multiple-choice, true/false, gap-fill and dictation tasks. These are called **objective tests**.
- Marking some kinds of tasks, e.g. compositions, role-plays, stories, interviews, involves judging many things together, e.g. for writing: spelling, handwriting, punctuation, grammar, vocabulary, organisation of ideas, fluency of writing. The learner may do some of these things well but others poorly. The mark we give to the learners' answers in these kinds of tasks depends on our judgement. These tasks are called **subjective tests**.
- Another kind of assessment method is a **portfolio**. This is a collection of learners' work, which the learner creates him/herself, or with the teacher, during a course. Often it also contains comments on the work written by the learner or classmates. Portfolios can be used for formal or informal assessment.
- Some informal assessment methods are: observing learners' spoken or written work and answers to comprehension tasks; keeping notes on the learners' performance; asking learners to complete self- or peer-assessment sheets. We often use informal assessment methods to assess areas such as attitude and effort, particularly with young learners and teenagers. Informal assessment is often followed up by feedback to the learners on the strengths and weaknesses of their performance, and suggestions for how to improve.

## ■ Key concepts and the language teaching classroom

- Assessment can affect what we teach, how we teach and our learners' motivation for learning. It is very important for tests to have a good influence on teaching and learning.
- Some assessment tasks are easy to write and to mark. But do they reflect what we are teaching and what learners need to use the language for? We should not use a particular testing method just because it is easy to use and easy to mark.
- To really reflect the level of learners' learning, the content and methods of progress and achievement tests should reflect the content and methods of our teaching.
- Feedback to learners on what they got right or wrong, their strengths and weaknesses, and what they can do to improve, is very important. Through feedback, assessment helps learning.
- Informal assessment is often much more suitable for assessing young learners than formal assessment. This is because their ways of thinking and learning are based on experiencing and communicating.

See Unit 21 for including assessment in teaching and Units 28, 31 and 32 for correcting learners' work and giving feedback.

## FOLLOW-UP ACTIVITY *(See page 173 for answers)*

Here are ten assessment tasks. Can you name them and say what they aim to test?

1 The learner looks at a simple picture story, then tells the story to the teacher.
2 The learners listen to a recording describing the appearance of a girl. Then they complete a picture of the girl by drawing her.
3 Learners take part in a speaking activity in which they act out parts.
4 The learners answer some simple questions about themselves orally.
5 The learners complete blanks with the correct form of the verb *to have*.
6 The learners choose the correct words for some pictures, and write them under the pictures.
7 The learners repeat words after the teacher.
8 The learners research and write about a topic.
9 The learners fill in sheets about their own progress.
10 The teacher keeps notes on learners' difficulties with the area being taught, then discusses them with the learners.

## REFLECTION

1 How was your English assessed at school? Did assessment help you learn English?
2 Which are better assessments of a learner's English: tests that focus on communication or tests that focus on accuracy?
3 Which is more helpful to teaching and learning: informal or formal assessment?

## DISCOVERY ACTIVITIES

1 Look back to the reasons for assessment on page 71. Which kinds of assessment take place in your school?
2 Look at a test from your coursebook. Decide on its purpose. Does it use objective or subjective tasks? Does it focus on accuracy or communication? Does it match what and how you teach?
3 Think of one of your classes. What are you teaching them now? How could you carry out some informal assessment of this area of learning? Write your answers in your TKT portfolio.
4 Use the *TKT Glossary* to find the meaning of these terms: *cloze test, continuous assessment, matching task, open comprehension questions, oral test, sentence completion.*

............................................................................................

**TKT practice task** *(See page 176 for answers)*

For questions 1-5, match the instructions with the terms listed **A-F**. There is one extra option which you do not need to use.

Terms

> A labelling
> B jumbled sentences
> C picture composition
> D matching
> E gap-fill
> F discussion

Instructions

1 Read the sentences and complete the blanks with one word only.
2 What are the names of these things? Write the name beside each picture.
3 Draw a line between the words on the left and their meanings on the right.
4 Exchange ideas on the topic with your classmates.
5 Look at these and write the story they tell.

............................................................................................

*A sample answer sheet is on page 168.*

For questions **1-5**, match the example language with the grammatical terms listed **A-F**.

Mark the correct letter (**A-F**) on your answer sheet.

There is one extra option which you do not need to use.

| Example language | Grammatical terms |
|---|---|
| **1** my, your, our | **A** subject pronouns |
| **2** that, which, who | **B** possessive adjectives |
| **3** we, you, she | **C** prepositions of movement |
| **4** during, after, until | **D** relative pronouns |
| **5** through, along, towards | **E** prepositions of time |
| | **F** interrogative pronouns |

For questions **6-10**, choose the best option to complete each statement about the uses of grammatical structures.

Mark the correct letter (**A, B** or **C**) on your answer sheet.

**6** We use superlative forms of adjectives to

- A   describe equal things or people.
- B   show differences between groups of things or people.
- C   compare things or people to a whole group they are part of.

**7** We can use *will* to express

- A   obligation in the future.
- B   decisions about the future.
- C   fixed plans.

**8** We use the passive to

- A   say what happens to the subject of the sentence.
- B   show that the verb is not important.
- C   focus on the object of the verb.

9 | We use tag questions to

    A  show surprise.
    B  check that something is true.
    C  express obligation.

10 | We use conjunctions to

    A  link words or sentences.
    B  make topic sentences.
    C  make adjectives stronger.

For questions 11-16, match the examples of words with the lexical categories listed **A-G**.

Mark the correct letter (**A-G**) on your answer sheet.

There is one extra option which you do not need to use.

| Examples of words | Lexical categories |
|---|---|
| 11 trees, flowers, grass | A  idioms |
| 12 two, too; blue, blew; pair, pear | B  suffixes |
| 13 down in the mouth, green fingers, a pain in the neck | C  synonyms |
| 14 take off, give in, get out | D  lexical set |
| 15 calmly, nationality, childhood | E  prefixes |
| 16 lucky, fortunate; sad, miserable; awful, terrible | F  homophones |
| | G  phrasal verbs |

For questions 17-24, look at the following questions about phonology and the possible answers.

Choose the correct option **A**, **B** or **C**.

Mark the correct letter (**A**, **B** or **C**) on your answer sheet.

17 | Which is the correct phonemic script for *weekend*?

    A  /wiːkend/
    B  /wɪkend/
    C  /jiːkend/

18 Which option shows the correct word stress for *telephone*?

   A   telEphone
   B   TELephone
   C   telePHONE

19 What is a phoneme?

   A   The smallest sound.
   B   The smallest sound that has meaning.
   C   A symbol representing a sound.

20 What meaning does the main stress on <u>John</u> give to this sentence?
   I gave the book to <u>John</u>.

   A   I was the person who gave John the book.
   B   I only gave a book to John, nothing else.
   C   John was the person I gave the book to.

21 Which of the following ends with a consonant?

   A   banana
   B   carrot
   C   potato

22 What is a contraction?

   A   A shortened form of a word.
   B   Two words made into one.
   C   The first letters of several words.

23 Which of these words is stressed on the first syllable?

   A   re°stricted
   B   °paragraph
   C   substi°tution

24 In which of these words is the first letter a voiced sound?

   A   table
   B   forget
   C   dark

For questions **25-30**, match the example language with the functions listed **A-G**.

Mark the correct letter (**A-G**) on your answer sheet.

There is one extra option which you do not need to use.

| Example language | Functions |
|---|---|
| 25 I'm not sure if I'll go or not. | **A** persuading |
| 26 Please come with me. I really want you to. | **B** giving personal information |
| 27 What do you think of his idea? | **C** attracting attention |
| 28 I'm 15 next birthday. | **D** giving advice |
| 29 Can I stay out late tonight? | **E** expressing uncertainty |
| 30 Hey, listen, listen. | **F** asking for an opinion |
| | **G** asking for permission |

For questions **31-35**, match the speaker's words with the speaking subskills that he is talking about listed **A-F**.

Mark the correct letter (**A-F**) on your answer sheet.

There is one extra option which you do not need to use.

**Subskills**

| | |
|---|---|
| **A** | connecting your ideas |
| **B** | interacting |
| **C** | pronouncing accurately |
| **D** | using language accurately |
| **E** | speaking fluently |
| **F** | using language appropriately |

**Speaker's words**

31 Sometimes I hesitate a lot or speak extremely slowly.

32 I always try to make eye contact with people when I speak to them.

33 You often need to use polite language when you meet people in formal situations.

34 I was so tired that I made lots of mistakes in my grammar.

35 It's quite difficult to speak with the right accent, so they often don't understand me.

For questions 36-40, match the descriptions with the reading and writing subskills listed **A-F**.

Mark the correct letter (**A-F**) on your answer sheet.

There is one extra option which you do not need to use.

### Subskills

| | |
|---|---|
| A | extensive reading |
| B | handwriting |
| C | scanning |
| D | editing |
| E | skimming |
| F | planning |

### Descriptions

36 You read things really quickly – just to find specific information.

37 Before you write long texts, like essays, you work out which order to present your ideas in.

38 You go through some parts of long texts slowly and carefully and through others quickly.

39 You need to learn to shape your letters correctly.

40 You often need to read what you've written and change it to make it easier to understand.

For questions 41-45, match the descriptions of the learners' preferred ways of learning with the learning styles listed **A-C**.

Mark the correct letter (**A-C**) on your answer sheet.

You need to use some options more than once.

### Learning styles

| | |
|---|---|
| A | Conformists: these learners prefer to learn about language rather than communicate. They like depending on the teacher. |
| B | Concrete learners: they enjoy the social aspects of learning and learning from experience. |
| C | Reflective learners: they prefer to have the opportunity to think carefully about their answers before giving them. |

### Preferred ways of learning

The learner likes:

41 doing role-plays and writing letters to real people.

42 having quiet time to analyse problems.

43 working through a grammar book with guidance.

44 going to the centre of town to chat to tourists.

45 having time to edit his work before giving it to the teacher.

For questions **46-50**, match the teacher's decisions with the considerations about learning listed **A-C**.

Mark the correct letter (**A-C**) on your answer sheet.

### Considerations about learning

| | |
|---|---|
| A | the role of errors |
| B | motivation |
| C | learning style |

### Teacher's decisions

46 The teacher decides not to correct the learners during a fluency activity.

47 The teacher decides to sing a song with the class who are disappointed with their test results.

48 The teacher decides to let one learner work by himself as he works better that way.

49 The teacher decides to read the class a story they all really like.

50 The teacher encourages learners to ask for clarification when they don't understand one another.

For questions 51-55, choose the best option to complete each statement about language learning.

Mark the correct letter (**A**, **B** or **C**) on your answer sheet.

---

51 Interlanguage is

    A   a language only learners use.
    B   a language like English.
    C   a language just used by children.

52 L1 learners process language

    A   after they fully realise what it means.
    B   until they can use it correctly and appropriately.
    C   because they try to avoid making mistakes.

53 When L2 learners overgeneralise new language they

    A   need to be corrected quickly.
    B   are experimenting with language.
    C   are not paying attention to grammar.

54 Developmental errors

    A   cannot be avoided.
    B   block the language learning process.
    C   help learners understand correct grammar.

55 Both L1 and L2 learners

    A   make errors due to interference.
    B   focus frequently on the form of language.
    C   pick up language from their surroundings.

For questions 56-63, match the coursebook activities with the terms listed **A-I**.

Mark the correct letter (**A-I**) on your answer sheet.

There is one extra option which you do not need to use.

**Terms**

| | |
|---|---|
| A | information gap |
| B | free writing |
| C | brainstorming |
| D | role-play |
| E | jumbled text |
| F | multiple-choice |
| G | form filling |
| H | prioritising |
| I | *wh-* comprehension questions |

**Coursebook activities**

**56**
Read the text and choose the best description of the children.
a) The children played with the ball.
b) The children didn't want to play with the ball.
c) The children couldn't find the ball.

**57**

| Card A | Card B |
|---|---|
| Talk to your partner and find out about his/her family. | Answer your partner's questions and find out about his/her hobbies. |

**58**
Here is a list of eight objects you might need on a seaside holiday. With your partner, number them 1–8 for how important they are to take with you.

toothpaste     sunglasses     a good book     your mobile phone

a camera     your credit card     a guidebook     a swimsuit

**59**
The paragraphs in this story are in the wrong order. Read them and number them in the correct order.

**60** Complete the blanks with information about yourself.

Name: ................. Age: .................

Address: ................. Nationality: .................

Favourite activity(ies): ................. Name of best friend: .................

**61** Listen to the conversation and then write answers to these questions:
a) Where does the boy live? .................
b) When does he get up? .................
c) Who does he often play with? .................
d) How does he get to school? .................
e) Why does he like going to school? .................

**62**

| Card A | Card B |
|---|---|
| You are lost. Ask a passer-by the way to the National Museum. | You are in Nathan Street. A tourist asks you the way to the National Museum. Tell him/her the way. |

**63** With a partner, make a list of all the words you know about food.

For questions **64-69**, look at the following descriptions of assessment activities and three possible terms for each one.

Choose the correct option **A, B or C**.

Mark the correct letter (**A, B or C**) on your answer sheet.

**64** The learners listen to two classmates carrying out a role-play and then give them feedback on their performance.

A a subjective test    B teacher assessment    C peer assessment

**65** The teacher monitors two learners in her class carrying out a role-play. She takes notes on their performance.

A a placement test    B informal assessment    C a diagnostic test

**66** At the end of term the learners look at their written work, select some of it and put it in a folder for the teacher to grade.

A formative assessment    B a progress test    C a portfolio

67 The learners do a gap-fill exercise for which there is only one answer for each gap.

    **A** an achievement test      **B** an objective test      **C** continuous assessment

68 The learners answer questions guiding them to assess and grade their own compositions.

    **A** an oral test      **B** formal assessment      **C** self-assessment

69 The learners do a test to see how good they are at English in general.

    **A** a written test      **B** a cloze test      **C** a proficiency test

For questions **70-74**, match the teacher's words with the purposes of the presentation activities listed **A-F**.

Mark the correct letter (**A-F**) on your answer sheet.

There is one extra option which you do not need to use.

**Purposes of the presentation activities**

| | |
|---|---|
| A | setting the context |
| B | concept checking |
| C | explaining meaning |
| D | focusing on pronunciation |
| E | using aids to convey meaning |
| F | drilling |

**Teacher's words**

70 Can you give me another word with the same meaning?

71 Listen. The stress is on the fourth syllable: 'accommoDAtion'.

72 We use it to clean our teeth.

73 Today we're going to talk about inventions.

74 Look, here's a picture of one.

For questions **75-80**, match the classroom activities with their main teaching purposes listed **A-G**.

Mark the correct letter (**A-G**) on your answer sheet.

There is one extra option which you do not need to use.

| Classroom activities | Teaching purposes |
|---|---|
| 75 Helping learners to use dictionaries | A giving controlled practice |
| 76 Class discussion | B developing understanding of coherence and cohesion |
| 77 Lead-in | C developing listening skills |
| 78 Vocabulary quiz | D giving fluency practice |
| 79 Jumbled paragraphs | E introducing the topic of a lesson |
| 80 Substitution drill | F developing learner autonomy |
| | G revising |

## Module 2 | Lesson planning and use of resources for language teaching

### Part 1 | Planning and preparing a lesson or sequence of lessons
### Unit 18 | Identifying and selecting aims

■ How do we identify and select aims?

**Aims** are what we want learners to learn or be able to do at the end of a lesson, a **sequence** (i.e. a series) of lessons or a whole course. Aims may focus, for example, on a **function** or a **grammatical structure**, on the vocabulary of a particular topic or on developing a language **skill**. Aims, especially for younger learners, may not always focus on particular areas of language. The aim of a lesson may also be listening to a story for pleasure or encouraging a positive attitude towards the foreign language. To identify and select the most appropriate aims, we need to ask ourselves two questions:

What do my learners already know?

What do they need to know?

The answers to these questions will help us to make sure that the aims are the right ones for a particular group of learners at a particular time.

■ Key concepts

Look at the table. Can you work out what the difference is between main aims, subsidiary aims and personal aims?

| Main aim | Subsidiary aims | Personal aims |
|---|---|---|
| To practise making polite requests in the context of making holiday arrangements.<br>Example **exponent**: *Could you give me some information about hotels?* | Grammar: to revise modal auxiliary verbs.<br>Functional exponents: *Could/Would you ...?*<br>Vocabulary: to consolidate **lexis** for travel, accommodation.<br>Phonology: to focus on **intonation.**<br>Speaking: to give controlled oral practice. | To improve my organisation of the whiteboard; to give clearer examples. |

A **main aim**, like the one above, describes the most important thing we want to achieve in a lesson or sequence of lessons. For example, we may want learners to understand and practise using new language; to **reinforce** or **consolidate** (i.e. to make stronger) the use of language they already know by giving them further practice; or to revise language they have recently learnt. On a lesson plan the main aim should also include an example of the target language we are planning to teach.

As well as a main aim, a lesson may also have **subsidiary aims**. Subsidiary aims show the language or skills learners must be able to use well in order to achieve the main aim of the lesson. In the example on page 86, the main aim is to practise making polite requests; the subsidiary aims describe the language and skill that learners will need to make these requests. Stating both main and subsidiary aims is a good way of making sure that our lesson plan focuses on what we want our learners to learn, or to be able to do. It enables us to see how the lesson should develop, from one **stage** (or part) to the next, building up our learners' knowledge or skills in the best possible order.

In addition to learning aims for the learners, we may also want to think about our own personal aims as teachers. **Personal aims** show what we would like to improve or focus on in our own teaching. Like the ones in the table on page 86, these might be about improving the way that we handle aids and materials or particular teaching techniques, or they might be about our relationship with the learners. Here are some more examples:

- to try different correction techniques
- to remember to check instructions
- to write more clearly on the blackboard/whiteboard
- to make more use of the **phonemic chart** (a poster with **phonemic symbols**)
- to get learners to work with different partners
- to get quieter learners to answer questions.

Identifying and selecting aims are the first steps in planning a lesson. Once we have decided on the aims, we can design or select the most appropriate activities, put them in the best order and choose the most suitable **teaching aids** (things we can use to support our teaching in the classroom) and materials. After the lesson, we can look back at this part of the plan to see whether we have **achieved** our **aims**, i.e. whether we have succeeded in teaching what we planned to teach. This also helps us to select the most appropriate aims for future lessons.

## Key concepts and the language teaching classroom

- The **syllabus** (i.e. the course programme) and/or the coursebook will give us a general direction for planning our teaching. To decide on specific aims for a particular lesson, however, we should think about our learners' needs and the stage they have reached in their learning.
- We can identify and select appropriate personal aims in a similar way, i.e. by looking back at earlier lessons we have taught and thinking about things that worked well and things we want to improve.
- We should not confuse aims and **procedures**. Aims describe what the learners will learn or what they will be able to do with the language, while procedures – for example, listening to a recording and answering questions about it – are what the teacher and learners will do at each stage of the lesson.
- Aims should not be too general. 'To teach the past simple' or 'to develop learners' reading skills' do not say enough about the purpose of the lesson. More specific aims might be 'to introduce and practise the past simple for talking about personal experiences' or 'to give learners practice in **predicting** content, **scanning** for specific information and guessing meaning from **context**'.

- We shouldn't plan to do too much in a lesson. The amount we plan to cover will depend on the length of the lesson and the learners' level.
- Learners also need to know what the lesson is going to be about. It is often helpful to announce our aims (or to write them up on the board) at the beginning of the lesson, and/or to repeat them at the end.
- Learners of all ages find it helpful to know why they are doing things. For younger learners the aims of a lesson can be described in very simple language, focusing on the things they will do in the lesson and the language knowledge they will take away from it. (For example, 'Today we're going to read a story and learn how to describe people in English'.)

*See Unit 19 for identifying the different components of a lesson plan, Unit 20 for planning an individual lesson or a sequence of lessons and Units 23–25 for the selection and use of materials, activities and aids.*

**FOLLOW-UP ACTIVITY** *(See page 173 for answers)*

The procedures in the table below show a sequence of activities for a lesson with the main aim of developing intermediate students' confidence and skill in informal conversation. The subsidiary aims for the lesson (A–H) are in the wrong order. Put them in the right order so that they match the correct procedures.

| Procedure | Subsidiary aims |
|---|---|
| 1 Students move around the classroom to find students with matching halves of sentences. | A • to give students fluency practice • to practise using target language in a meaningful context |
| 2 They talk in pairs about what they find difficult in listening to informal conversation. | B • to develop peer correction skills |
| 3 They hear an informal conversation and identify speakers, place and situation. | C • to listen for detailed information • to focus students' attention on target language |
| 4 They listen again and fill in missing phrases in the transcript. | D • to practise gist listening • to create a context |
| 5 Repetition drill: students practise key phrases. Pairs practise simple two-line exchanges using key phrases. | E • to get students actively involved • to put students into pairs |
| 6 Pairs write and practise their own conversation from role cards, using key phrases where possible. Several pairs perform and record conversations. | F • to give students confidence in speaking through controlled practice |
| 7 Class comment and suggest improvements to grammar and vocabulary. | G • to review the whole lesson • to give the teacher feedback |
| 8 Students discuss what they have learnt. | H • to raise awareness of what the lesson aim will be • to encourage personal involvement |

## REFLECTION

Think about these comments from teachers. Which do you agree with and why?

1 I often discover what my aims are while I am teaching the lesson. Sometimes I only find out when the lesson is over.
2 Learners don't want to know about aims. They just want to get on with the lesson.
3 My coursebook always tells me what my aims should be.

## DISCOVERY ACTIVITIES

1 Look at the teacher's book for your coursebook. Does it describe the aims of units and/or lessons? If so, do you think they are appropriate for your learners? Make notes in your TKT portfolio.
2 In your portfolio, list your main aims, subsidiary aims and personal aims for the last lesson you taught and the next one you are planning for the same class.
3 For useful ideas about selecting and describing aims, have a look at:
   Chapter 6, Section 5 of *Learning Teaching* by Jim Scrivener (2nd edition, Macmillan 2005), the first section ('Planning') of *Action Plan for Teachers – A Guide to Teaching English* by Callum Robertson with Richard Acklam, downloadable free from:
   http://www.teachingenglish.org.uk/download/books_notes/Action_Plan.pdf
4 Use the *TKT Glossary* to find the meaning of these terms: *highlight, stimulate discussion*.
5 Can you match the verbs and nouns listed below to make three phrases that describe teaching aims? Use the *TKT Glossary* to check your answers.
   raise      confidence
   arouse     awareness
   give       interest

........................................................................

**TKT practice task** *(See page 176 for answers)*

For questions 1-7, match the lesson summaries with the lesson aims listed **A-H**.
There is one extra option which you do not need to use.

_____

**Lesson summaries**

1  Learners put jumbled sections of a text in order. The teacher focuses on conjunctions, time expressions, pronouns, etc. Learners make notes on a similar topic, and then they produce a similar text.

2  Learners look at a town map and discuss the best route from the station to a hotel, and then they listen to a conversation on cassette and compare their route with the one on the cassette.

3  In pairs, learners read different texts about soldiers' duties, and then they exchange information about them. Pairs work together to complete lists of rules for soldiers, using *must*, *should*, *doesn't/don't have to*.

4  Learners brainstorm vocabulary and ideas on the topic, and then in groups they draft the text for a leaflet to advertise their town to tourists. Groups then exchange texts to make corrections and/or suggest improvements.

5  Learners listen to a dialogue and identify the tense the speakers use to talk about future arrangements. The teacher checks understanding. Learners do repetition drills, and then they practise using the structure in a guided role-play.

6  Learners work in large groups to brainstorm ideas on different roles, and then form new groups for a role-based discussion. The teacher monitors the discussion.

7  Learners match words with pictures, and build up word maps, which they compare and develop. Then they work together to produce entries for a class dictionary.

**Lesson aims**

A  to practise listening for detail
B  to practise writing for a communicative purpose
C  to present and provide controlled practice of the present progressive
D  to revise and practise modal auxiliary verbs
E  to train learners to learn autonomously
F  to give learners oral fluency practice
G  to raise awareness of how to join sentences and paragraphs
H  to revise and consolidate vocabulary

........................................................................

# Unit 19    Identifying the different components of a lesson plan

## How do we identify the different components of a lesson plan?

Choose the comparison that you think best describes a lesson plan.

A lesson plan is like ... an instruction leaflet      a photograph      a story      a road map
a computer programme      a series of road signs      a written summary      something else?

A lesson plan is a set of notes that helps us to think through what we are going to teach and how we are going to teach it. It also guides us during and after the lesson. We can identify the most important components of a lesson plan by thinking carefully about *what* we want our learners to do and *how* we want them to do it.

The main components of a lesson plan show us what the lesson is for (the **aims**) and what the teacher and the learners will do during the lesson and how they will do it (the **procedures**). Other components help us to think about possible problems and remind us of things we need to remember about the learners. So a lesson plan is most like a road map or a series of road signs, i.e. something that shows us where we are going and how we are going to get there – although we may sometimes find that during the journey we have to take a different route!

Here are some ways a lesson plan helps the teacher.

| Before the lesson | Writing down the aims and the procedures for each **stage** of the lesson helps us to make sure that we have planned the best possible **sequence** to enable us to **achieve** those **aims**. |
|---|---|
| During the lesson | The plan can also help the teacher to check **timing** – the amount of time we plan for each stage – and to check that the lesson is following the sequence we decided on. |
| After the lesson | We can keep the plan as a record of what happened, making any changes necessary to show how the lesson was different from the plan. We can then use the plan and notes to help plan the next lesson. (At this stage, the plan may be more like a photograph, a story or a summary, giving us a record of the lesson.) |

# Key concepts

A lesson plan can include the following headings. Which ones do you think should always appear? Which ones may only appear sometimes?

| Lesson plan headings | |
|---|---|
| Level and number of learners | who we are planning the lesson for |
| Timetable fit | how the lesson is connected to the last lesson and/or the next one |
| **Main aim(s)** | what we want learners to learn or to be able to do by the end of the lesson |
| **Subsidiary aims** | other things we want learners to be able to do during the lesson because they lead to the main aim |
| **Personal aims** | aspects of our own teaching we want to develop or improve |
| **Assumptions** | what we think learners already know or can already do related to the aims |
| **Anticipated language problems** | things that learners may find difficult |
| Possible solutions | action we will take to deal with the anticipated problems |
| **Teaching aids**, materials, equipment | useful reminders of things to take to the lesson |
| Procedures | tasks and activities for each stage |
| Timing | length of time needed for each stage |
| **Interaction patterns** | ways in which learners work at different stages, i.e. individually, in pairs, in groups, as a whole class |
| Homework | |

It is usually a good idea to anticipate possible problems and solutions, but in a revision lesson we may not need these headings. Also, we may not have personal aims for every lesson, and we may not always give learners homework!

## ▪ Key concepts and the language teaching classroom

Look carefully at this example of part of a lesson plan which aims to introduce and practise language for giving advice. Then read the points below.

| Timing | Procedure | Subsidiary aims | Aids and materials | Interaction pattern |
|---|---|---|---|---|
| 5 minutes | Ask students who they ask for advice if they have a problem. | **Warmer/lead-in**: to get students talking and introduce the topic | – | Pairwork |
| 10 minutes | Discuss typical problems for young people; elicit language to ask for and give advice. | To create context<br>To revise modal auxiliary verbs<br>To elicit/introduce vocabulary | Magazine pictures<br>Whiteboard | Teacher →<br>whole class |
| 5 minutes | Show headlines for students to guess the content of letters to the advice page in a teen magazine. | To get students ready for reading<br>To predict content<br>To use students' own knowledge | OHP | Teacher →<br>whole class |
| 15 minutes | Students read different mini-texts, then summarise the content of the letters. | To check predictions<br>Intensive reading<br>To introduce the structure 'If I were you, I'd…' | Photocopies of six problem page letters | 1st group work<br>↓<br>2nd group work<br>(new groups) |

- When we make a lesson plan, we need to ask ourselves how the procedures we have planned will help to achieve our aims and to make sure there are strong connections between the different stages.
- We also need to consider **variety**, i.e. how we can use different activity types, language **skills** and interaction patterns. Learners of all ages need different activities in a lesson, but this is especially important for younger learners.
- During the lesson we should teach the learners, not the lesson plan! We must be prepared, if necessary, to change our plan while we are teaching. If we have a clear plan, we will be more aware of what we are changing and why. We can include some different possibilities in a lesson plan, e.g. an extra activity to use if learners take less time than expected to complete a **task**, and this can help if we are not sure how well parts of the plan will work.

*See Unit 18 for identifying and selecting aims and Unit 20 for planning an individual lesson or a sequence of lessons.*

**FOLLOW-UP ACTIVITY** *(See page 173 for answers)*

Some of the teacher's notes for this lesson plan are missing. Put the notes A–E in the correct places in the plan.

| Lesson plan headings | Teacher's notes |
|---|---|
| Timetable fit | 1 |
| Main aim(s) | 2 |
| Subsidiary aim(s) | 3 To listen for detail to a model story |
| Personal aim(s) | 4 |
| Assumptions | 5 Students can already form tenses accurately |
| Anticipated language problems | 6 Students may use present tenses |
| Possible solution | 7 |
| Procedures | 8 |

A  To enable students to use past tenses accurately and put events in order in simple narratives
B  Students listen to the model story, then in groups, plan and write their own stories
C  Use gestures to remind students to use past tenses
D  To follow on from work on past tenses and to prepare for the storytelling project
E  To make sure that board writing is clear and readable

**REFLECTION**

Think about these comments from teachers. Which do you agree with and why?
1  Written lesson plans are helpful when you first start teaching, but experienced teachers don't need them. I plan all my lessons in my head.
2  Lesson plans don't help me teach because I always try to respond to learners' needs during the lesson.
3  Writing a lesson plan is the important thing. I always have a written plan, but often I don't look at it while I'm teaching.

## DISCOVERY ACTIVITIES

1 Try out different ways of writing lesson plans – e.g. in columns, on cards – to find out which style suits you best. Have a look at Chapter 8 ('Why did I do it like this?') of *Children Learning English* by Jayne Moon, Macmillan 2000, for some useful examples.

2 In your TKT portfolio, collect examples of plans you write for different kinds of lessons. Also write comments on what the strong and weaker points of the lesson were, and what you would change next time.

3 For some good ideas about lesson planning, read two short articles on planning by Callum Robertson, BBC English at:
http://www.teachingenglish.org.uk/think/methodology/planning1.shtml and
http://www.teachingenglish.org.uk/think/methodology/planning2.shtml

4 For more detailed advice on planning and further examples of how to write a plan, look at Chapter 22, Sections A, B1–3 and C of *The Practice of English Language Teaching* (third edition) by Jeremy Harmer, Pearson Education Ltd 2001 and Chapter 8 of *Teaching Practice Handbook* (second edition) by Roger Gower, Diane Phillips and Steve Walters, Macmillan 1995.

5 For lesson plans on a wide variety of topics that you can download free, visit:
http://www.in2english.com/teaching

**TKT practice task** *(See page 176 for answers)*

For questions 1-7, match the stages of the lesson with the subsidiary aims listed **A-H**.
There is one extra option which you do not need to use.

### Lesson stages

1 Check vocabulary from the last lesson.
2 Introduce the topic and elicit/present new words and phrases.
3 Learners reorder jumbled paragraphs of a text.
4 Learners match words in the text with possible meanings.
5 Learners answer true/false questions.
6 Learners underline examples of reported speech.
7 Learners exchange texts and give feedback.

### Subsidiary aims

A focus on form
B deducing meaning from context
C peer correction
D check detailed comprehension
E contextualise and pre-teach vocabulary
F check learners' awareness of text organisation (pronouns, linking, etc.)
G controlled practice of target structure
H revise language already learnt

# Unit 20    Planning an individual lesson or a sequence of lessons

- ## How do we plan an individual lesson or a sequence of lessons?

When we plan an individual lesson, we need to think about its aims, the 'shape' of the lesson and the kind of techniques that are most appropriate for a particular group of learners. For example, if we are introducing a new grammatical structure, we might choose a **Presentation, Practice and Production** (**PPP**) approach or a **Task-based Learning** (**TBL**) approach. **Skills** lessons, too, have regular shapes that we can use to organise lesson plans: for example, for receptive skills, we usually plan tasks or activities for learners to do before, while and after reading or listening; for productive skills, there is usually an introductory stage to **set the scene** (i.e. to explain the context) and a **feedback** stage after the speaking or writing activity.

We also need to think about the connections between the aims of the lesson and the procedures we will use to achieve those aims. The available materials, the length of the lesson and the information we have about our learners will all help us to identify possible procedures. But the most important thing is to make sure that the materials, tasks and activities we select are the ones that will help a particular group of learners to achieve the aim we have identified.

A **sequence** of lessons is a number of related lessons that develop language knowledge and/or language skills over a period of time. Sequences may develop a single topic or language area, or may involve topics or language areas that are very closely connected. Here are three examples:

| *Structural sequence* | *Integrated skills sequence* | *Project work* |
|---|---|---|
| 1  revision: past simple<br>2  revision: present perfect<br>3  contrast: past simple vs. present perfect | 1  vocabulary development: describing places (**function**: describing)<br>2  reading: choosing a holiday<br>3  writing: letter to a friend narrating holiday experiences (function: narrating) | 1  reading and listening about free time activities<br>2  class **survey** and research: sport and entertainment<br>3  preparation of a poster display to show results of survey |

# Key concepts

*Planning an individual lesson*
When we plan an individual lesson, we have to ask ourselves a number of questions:

- Will the topic be interesting and motivating for my learners?
- Are the activities and teaching materials at the right level for all the learners?
- Have I planned enough for the time available? Do I need any extra material?
- Have I planned too much for the time available? Are there any stages I can cut if necessary?
- Have I thought about exactly how to start and end the lesson?
- Does each step in the lesson help to achieve the aim?

*Planning a sequence of lessons*
Look at these three teachers' **schemes of work** (i.e. outline plans) for a sequence of four lessons. What do you think might be the advantages and disadvantages of each scheme?

|        | Scheme A | Scheme B | Scheme C |
|--------|----------|----------|----------|
| Week 3 | • Grammar<br>• Vocabulary | • Grammar revision (past tenses)<br>• Vocabulary (free time activities)<br>• Practice exercise (from coursebook) | • Class discussion of advantages and disadvantages of living in the city<br>• Revise and extend vocabulary<br>• Focus on comparative and superlative adjectives and adverbs; practice exercise |
| Week 4 | • Listening<br>• Speaking | • Check vocabulary<br>• Reading (emails)<br>• Speaking – **fluency** activities | • Reading: personal stories: students order sections of text<br>• Focus on text organisation<br>• Writing: students' own stories<br>• **Peer correction** (where students correct one another) |
| Week 5 | • Reading<br>• Writing | • Quick revision: work from Weeks 3 and 4<br>• Listening (e.g. holiday story)<br>• Grammar focus (reported speech)<br>• Writing (report of story) | • Listening: song – group transcription<br>• Grammar game (snakes and ladders) to revise work on comparatives and superlatives<br>• Pronunciation practice: focus on /ə/ |
| Week 6 | • Test | • Speaking (**role-play**)<br>• Feedback | • Review of grammar and topic<br>• Group work: producing sections of tourist brochure for students' town |

A scheme of work helps us plan a sequence of lessons in the best way to cover the school **syllabus** or the units of a coursebook in the time available. It also helps us to think about what we want to achieve and what materials we might need. It also helps us to include enough variety across our lessons. Teacher and learners need clear **aims** beyond the single lesson and need to see how lessons are linked to each other. Here are some of the main advantages and disadvantages of the three schemes of work on page 97:

| Scheme | Advantages | Disadvantages |
|---|---|---|
| A | Leaves teacher free to respond to learners' needs. | Gives no details of what will happen in these lessons and so does not remind the teacher of general aims or what materials to prepare. |
| B | Quite detailed. Some sense of direction. | Probably the most useful of the three schemes of work. Not too much detail or too little, but the teacher will probably need to return to it and add more detail week by week to turn it into a set of lesson plans. |
| C | Very detailed. Gives very clear sense of direction. | Difficult to predict several weeks ahead exactly what learners' needs may be, so the teacher will need to return frequently to the scheme of work and change it if necessary. |

You can see that schemes of work are less detailed than lesson plans. Like any individual lesson, a sequence of lessons should have a logical and learning-friendly progression and a good balance of approaches and activities. Like a lesson plan, a scheme of work helps us to identify our aims and make sure we choose materials and **procedures** that match those aims.

## Key concepts and the language teaching classroom

- It's a good idea to make lesson plans look as simple as possible, so notes are better than full sentences, and there's no need to describe every step in great detail. However, we may want to write down some important things in a complete form – for example, prompts for drilling, questions to check learners' understanding, instructions, etc.
- A lesson plan should be clear and easy to read during the lesson. Different colours, boxes, underlining, etc. are useful. It is often helpful to include drawings of the way the blackboard (or whiteboard) will look at different stages.
- **Variety** is very important both in a sequence of lessons and in a single lesson. We should avoid always doing the same kinds of things in the same order, e.g. always beginning the lesson with a conversation or always ending with a role-play. There are several different ways of introducing variety into lessons. Here is a list of things we can **vary**:

| | |
|---|---|
| **pace** | → quick and fast-moving or slow and reflective |
| **interaction pattern** | → individual, pairs, groups, whole class |
| skill | → **productive** or **receptive** |
| level of difficulty | → non-demanding or requiring effort and concentration |
| content | → changing from one language point to another; from one subject to another |
| mood | → light or serious; happy or sad; tense or relaxed |
| exciting or calming activities | → 'stirring' (lively and active) or 'settling' (quietening down) |

(adapted from *A Course in Language Teaching* by Penny Ur, Cambridge University Press 1996)

- Learners may well require more frequent revision than the coursebook provides. A scheme of work is a good way to make sure that we **recycle** language (i.e. use it again) and include regular revision activities during a sequence of lessons.
- Coursebook units are often arranged around a specific topic (such as sport or relationships), which may be a useful way of linking together a sequence of lessons. This kind of sequence gives us the chance to develop particular areas of vocabulary, but learners may feel that the lessons are repetitive, so we need plenty of variety of texts and **tasks**.

*See Units 5–8 for skills-based lessons, Unit 18 for identifying and selecting aims and Unit 19 for identifying the different components of a lesson plan.*

**FOLLOW-UP ACTIVITIES** *(See page 174 for answers)*

1   The lesson summaries 1–6 below are part of a scheme of work to introduce and practise language for describing people, clothes and places. Complete the scheme of work with the correct summaries (A, B or C) for lessons 1, 5 and 6.

| |
|---|
| A Project work: groups prepare poster displays (magazine photographs)<br>   Writing: descriptions of people and places (further practice of functional language) |
| B Listening: descriptions of people<br>   Present new vocabulary and check pronunciation: lexical sets for describing people (flashcards and board drawings)<br>   Writing: descriptions of students in class |
| C Video (TV police drama): focus on descriptions of people<br>   Role-play in pairs: police interviews (practice of new language) → whole-class correction |

| |
|---|
| *Scheme of work* |
| 1 ................................................................................................................. |
| 2 Reading: descriptions of clothes (from teenage magazine)<br>   Vocabulary: dictionary work<br>   Writing: descriptions of people and clothes → peer correction (pairwork) |
| 3 Vocabulary: descriptions of places and people (photographs)<br>   Practice exercises (coursebook)<br>   Speaking: describe-and-draw activity (pairwork)<br>   Writing: descriptions of places drawn in speaking activity |
| 4 Vocabulary: pictures of people, clothes and places<br>   Grammar: comparative and superlative adjectives<br>   Practice exercises (coursebook)<br>   Speaking: general knowledge quiz (whole class) |
| 5 ................................................................................................................. |
| 6 ................................................................................................................. |

2    In the scheme of work in Activity 1, which lesson or lessons:

A  has/have a variety of pace?
B  use(s) different interaction patterns?
C  practise(s) receptive skills?
D  practise(s) productive skills?
E  increase(s) the level of difficulty?
F  has/have a change of topic?
G  has/have a change of language focus?
H  is/are lively and active?
I   is/are calm and quiet?

## REFLECTION

Think about these comments from teachers. Which do you agree with and why?
1  The coursebook gives me everything I need to plan a sequence of lessons.
2  If I do a scheme of work, I don't have to spend so much time planning individual lessons.
3  I want to respond to my learners' needs from lesson to lesson. A scheme of work stops me from doing that.

## DISCOVERY ACTIVITIES

1  Design a scheme of work for your next few lessons. Then summarise the aims of your sequence of lessons as a handout for learners or a poster for the classroom wall. Put a copy in your TKT portfolio.
2  For some very practical ideas on planning, look at Chapter 7 of *Planning Lessons and Courses* by Tessa Woodward, Cambridge University Press 2001 and *Planning Classwork*: *A Task-based Approach* by Sheila Estaire and Javier Zanón, Macmillan 1994.
3  Project work is a good way of planning a motivating sequence of lessons with plenty of variety. For ideas on planning project work and some good examples, have a look at this website:
   http://www.teachingenglish.org.uk/think/methodology/project_work.shtml
4  Use the *TKT Glossary* to find the meanings of these terms: *guided discovery, student-centred, teacher-centred*.

**TKT practice task** *(See page 176 for answers)*

For questions 1-5, look at the lessons in the project work sequence below and fill in the missing lessons from the options listed **A-E**.

A  Some learners look for information on the Internet or in the library and make notes; some plan surveys to find out information from others using questionnaires.
B  Groups exchange their work, check it and make final suggestions for editing.
C  In each group learners read each other's work, and make suggestions for editing.
D  Groups plan their work and decide how to share tasks.
E  Learners plan their writing or carry out survey interviews.

**Project work sequence**

| Aim: for learners to produce a class magazine |
| --- |
| • Explain project aims; whole class decides on list of topics; form interest groups |
| 1  ............................................................................................................ |
| 2  ............................................................................................................ |
| 3  ............................................................................................................ |
| • Learners write their first drafts. |
| 4  ............................................................................................................ |
| 5  ............................................................................................................ |
| • Make copies of the magazine for other classes to read. |

# Unit 21  Choosing assessment activities

## How do we choose assessment activities?

**Assessment** means collecting information about learners' performance in order to make judgements about their learning. We may choose to assess formally (through tests and examinations) or informally. We can carry out **informal assessment** during a lesson by **monitoring** (i.e. listening carefully) and observing learners while they are doing ordinary classroom activities. Informal assessment is an important way of checking how our learners are getting on, but of course we can't assess all our learners all the time during lessons. To get more information about the progress of individual learners, we also need to carry out **formal assessment** (e.g. a class test).

   When planning assessment, we need to think first about our reasons for assessing learners. Then we can decide when and how often to assess them, and choose what methods of assessment we are going to use.

## Key concepts

What are the differences between formal and informal assessment?

We can summarise the differences between formal and informal assessment under the headings of assessment tasks, marking and purpose:

| | *Formal assessment* | *Informal assessment* |
|---|---|---|
| *Assessment tasks* | • tests<br>• examinations | • normal classroom teaching and learning activities<br>• homework tasks |
| *Marking* | • learners receive grades (%, A–F, Pass/Fail, etc.) | • teacher keeps records of progress but does not give grades |
| *Purpose* | • to assess overall language ability (**proficiency test**)<br>• to assess learning at the end of a course (**achievement test**)<br>• to assess learning at the end of part of a course (**progress test**)<br>• to decide if learners can continue to the next level | • **feedback** for the teacher (i.e. to find out how successful our teaching has been)<br>• to help us improve our **procedures** or choose different materials or activities for future lessons<br>• feedback for learners about what they can do and what they still need to work on |

# Key concepts and the language teaching classroom

*Formal assessment*

- Formal assessment can consist of tasks with single answers (e.g. **multiple-choice questions**, **matching task**, **true/false questions**) that are easy to mark. **Objective test** tasks like these will give us information about learners' knowledge of particular language items and specific areas of language skills. Some formal assessment makes use of more real-life tasks, such as oral interviews, letters and essays, to get information about learners' general ability to use spoken and written language.
- When we prepare a class test, it is important to include a number of different tasks, so that we get a good picture of our learners' strengths and weaknesses, and to test the main things we have taught.
- We need to choose assessment tasks very carefully for young learners, making sure that the tasks are familiar and not too difficult or too abstract.

*Informal assessment*

- The amount of informal assessment we do depends on a number of things:
  - the size of the class
  - the age of the learners (informal assessment is especially useful for young learners for whom formal test tasks are often too abstract)
  - the language knowledge or skills we want to assess
  - the frequency of formal tests or examinations.
- It is important for learners to know that we are assessing them, and to know how and when we are doing it.
- To carry out informal assessment of **productive skills** in larger classes, we probably need to assess small numbers of learners in different lessons. We can record our opinions on a record sheet or fill in a check list.
- We can carry out informal assessment of **receptive skills** by checking learners' answers to reading or listening tasks, and taking notes on their performance.
- We can make separate assessments of learners' grammatical and lexical knowledge by using language games or quizzes, or by monitoring practice activities and making a note of frequent **errors**. We can then give feedback to individuals or to the whole class, or return to the problems later in a revision lesson.
- We may also wish to assess other things such as **motivation** and effort. We can do this by observation and also by talking to learners about their learning.
- It is important to keep records of informal assessment, especially in larger classes, so that we have the information we need to report or give feedback on our learners' progress. These records can be quite simple, with headings for, e.g. grammar, vocabulary, language skills, motivation and general progress against each learner's name.
- We need to plan informal assessment in the same way as we plan our teaching.

*Formal and informal assessment*

- We may use some of the same methods for both formal and informal assessment (e.g. assessing learners' spoken language in an interview). In the case of productive skills, whether the assessment is formal or informal, we need to judge learners' performance against clear descriptions of different levels of skill. These may be general descriptions of speaking or writing, or they may give separate descriptions of different **subskills**. Here are two examples for speaking. They are designed to assess a wide range of ability.

*Example 1*

| | |
|---|---|
| 5 | Speaks very well – very few errors. |
| 4 | Speaks quite well – some errors, but message is always clear. |
| 3 | Has some difficulties in speaking – frequent errors and not always clear. |
| 2 | Has serious problems in speaking – only very limited ability to communicate. |
| 1 | Almost unable to communicate. |

*Example 2*

| | *Accuracy* | *Fluency* | *Pronunciation* |
|---|---|---|---|
| 5 | Grammatical and lexical **accuracy** extremely high. | Speaks fluently without hesitation or searching for words. | Very clear; **stress** and **intonation** help to make meaning clear. |
| 4 | Quite accurate; some errors, but meaning is always clear. | Some hesitation and sometimes has to search for words. | Generally clear; reasonable control of stress and intonation. |
| 3 | Frequent errors; meaning is not always clear. | Quite hesitant; limited range of vocabulary and structures. | Frequent errors; not always clear enough to understand. |
| 2 | Very frequent errors; difficulty in making meaning clear. | Extremely hesitant; very limited range of language available. | Very frequent errors; often very difficult to understand. |
| 1 | Almost unable to communicate. | | |

*See Unit 17 for assessment types and tasks.*

## FOLLOW-UP ACTIVITY  *(See page 174 for answers)*

Read the following statements and decide whether they are true (T) or false (F).

1 We can use homework tasks for informal assessment.
2 Objective tests have many different possible answers, and this makes them difficult to mark.
3 In the best formal tests learners should only have to do a few different tasks.
4 It's important for learners to know when we are assessing them informally.
5 We can sometimes use games and quizzes for informal assessment.
6 The methods we use for formal assessment are always different from those we use for informal assessment.

## REFLECTION

Think about these comments from teachers. Which do you agree with and why?

1 I don't have time for informal assessment. I'm far too busy teaching.
2 Most of my assessment is informal. It's much better than formal testing as a way of finding out what my learners can do.
3 My learners have regular tests, so I don't need to do much informal assessment.

## DISCOVERY ACTIVITIES

1 Look at the next three units in your coursebook. What opportunities are there for informal assessment? In your TKT portfolio, keep a record of the assessment tasks you use.
2 For detailed information on ways of carrying out informal assessment, have a look at Chapters 1 and 2 of *Assessment* by Michael Harris and Paul McCann, Macmillan 1994 and 'Classroom Assessment' by Pauline Rea-Dickins, Chapter 11 in *Teaching and Learning in the Language Classroom* by Tricia Hedge, Oxford University Press 2000.
3 A language portfolio is a very good way of learners keeping a record of their own progress. An example is downloadable free, together with a Teacher's Guide, from: http://www.nacell.org.uk/resources/pub_cilt/portfolio.htm

**TKT practice task** (*See page 176 for answers*)

For questions 1-7, match the instructions for the assessment tasks with the assessment aims listed A-H.

There is one extra option which you do not need to use.

### Assessment aims

A  to assess oral fluency
B  to assess accurate pronunciation
C  to check knowledge of vocabulary
D  to check grammatical knowledge
E  to assess writing skills
F  to check awareness of stress
G  to check knowledge of functional exponents
H  to assess gist reading skills

### Instructions for assessment tasks

1 Use the notes to make complete sentences. Put the verbs into the correct form.
2 Choose the correct heading for each paragraph.
3 Reply to the advertisement, explaining why you are the best person for the job.
4 Find the words in the text which match the following definitions.
5 Discuss the problem with your partner and try to find the solution.
6 Choose the most appropriate response for each of the following situations.
7 Listen and underline the word that the speaker says most strongly.

# Part 2 | Selection and use of resources and materials

## Unit 22 | Consulting reference resources to help in lesson preparation

### ◼ How do we consult reference resources?

Reference resources are all the sources of information about language and about teaching that we can refer to for help in lesson preparation. They include **reference materials**, such as dictionaries and grammar books, books and articles about methodology in teachers' magazines, the **teacher's book** accompanying a coursebook that contains answers and teaching ideas, and websites on the Internet. Reference resources may also include people, for example, the Head of Department or colleagues who teach foreign languages or other subjects. We consult reference resources by knowing where we can find the information we need and how to find it.

### ◼ Key concepts

List as many reasons as you can think of for making use of reference resources.

When we are planning a lesson, there are many reasons for using reference resources. Some of the main ones are as follows:

*Checking the form and use of grammatical structures*
Some grammar books are written for teachers, with very detailed explanations. Others, designed for learners at different levels, use simpler language to give essential information about **grammatical structures**. Grammar books for learners can help us to see what information our learners need about grammatical structures and can provide us with suitable ways of describing or explaining grammar. The easiest books to use are those organised in alphabetical order, or which have a detailed index or table of contents. Some grammar books also include practice exercises, which teachers (and learners) often find useful.

*Checking the spelling, pronunciation and use of lexical items*
The most useful dictionaries for teachers to use themselves are advanced learners' dictionaries, which include example sentences, as well as information about the form and use of words. Most of these are also available on CD-ROM and online on publishers' websites. **Bilingual dictionaries** (which explain the meanings of words in the learner's own language), including electronic dictionaries, are useful when learners are looking for a word that they don't know in English. But these dictionaries usually give very little information about how to use a word, so it's a good idea for learners to check the words they find in a **monolingual dictionary** (i.e. one that explains the meanings of words in the language learners are learning). Learner dictionaries, like learner grammar books, can help teachers to find the most suitable ways of defining words and giving examples of their use.

*Developing your own understanding of language*

There are a number of books for teachers which aim to increase our **language awareness** (our understanding of how language works) and our awareness of how to teach language. They often include **tasks** that we can do by ourselves or with a colleague and detailed explanations and comments as well as answers.

*Anticipating learners' difficulties*

Reference materials about learners' **errors** can help us **anticipate** particular **language problems** that our learners might have. Many difficulties with vocabulary or grammar are the result of **interference** from **L1**. Books or articles about specific differences between the learner's L1 and English can help to explain these problems.

*Looking for new approaches to teaching lessons and new classroom activities*

If we are looking for new approaches or activities, or if we want to give our learners something different from their coursebook, there is a wide range of **supplementary materials** (i.e. materials you can use in addition to or instead of your coursebook), focusing on grammar, vocabulary and particular **skills**. There are also very many teacher's resource books with ideas and materials for all kinds of lessons. Some of these provide a wide range of activities for extra grammar or communicative practice, for example, while others focus on a particular type of classroom activity, such as dictation or storytelling. Most of these books have very clear indexes, giving information about **timing**, preparation, level, etc. There is also a growing number of free websites with articles for teachers on different teaching topics.

*Finding out how to use the material in your coursebook*

Teacher's books provide suggestions about how to use the material in the coursebook. Even if the lesson planning ideas in the teacher's book do not suit a particular teaching situation, it is still useful to look at these suggestions, as it may be possible to adapt them. Some teacher's books include different possible ways of planning a lesson, as well as explanations of answers to exercises and extra **resources** (i.e. things teachers can use to support their teaching in the classroom), such as homework tasks and activities for further practice.

*Getting advice about particular lessons or teaching materials*

Colleagues who have taught at the same level or used the same teaching materials may be able to offer useful advice. As with the suggestions in teacher's books, a colleague's approach may not suit us, but may help us to think about our own planning.

## Key concepts and the language teaching classroom

- Some grammar books and dictionaries may contain clearer explanations or examples. So when checking a language item, we should try to look at more than one reference resource.
- Language changes, as new words appear and people stop using some older words. Grammatical usage, too, changes slowly over time. One way to keep up to date is to use the most recently published grammar books and dictionaries.
- Dictionaries on CD-ROM have many extra features, such as practice activities, **collocation** searches and audio recordings of pronunciation.

- We can learn a great deal from other teachers' experiences. Many teachers' magazines include regular articles by teachers describing successful lessons they have taught.
- It may be easier to visit websites than to find the books and articles we need. There are many sites on the Internet where we can find free resources such as lesson plans, **worksheets** (pages with tasks and exercises on them that a teacher gives to learners during a lesson) and ideas for teaching. Some sites also offer simple programs for making classroom resources, such as crosswords and gap-fill exercises. The best way to find these materials is to visit one of the sites that has lists of links to useful teaching resources on the Internet.

## FOLLOW-UP ACTIVITY *(See page 174 for answers)*

Try to find resources 1–10 below. Then decide which type of resource (A–D) they are.

1 *A-Z of English Grammar and Usage* by Geoffrey Leech, Pearson Education Ltd 2001
2 *Cambridge Learner's Dictionary*, Cambridge University Press 2001
3 *Discussions That Work* by Penny Ur, Cambridge University Press 1981
4 *Planning from Lesson to Lesson* by Tessa Woodward and Seth Lindstromberg, Pearson Education Ltd 1995
5 http://www.ruthvilmi.net/hut/LangHelp/Grammar
6 *Working with Words* by Ruth Gairns and Stuart Redman, Cambridge University Press 1986
7 http://www.preschoolrainbow.org
8 *Motivating High-Level Learners* by David Cranmer, Pearson Education Ltd 1996
9 *Five-Minute Activities* by Penny Ur and Andrew Wright, Cambridge University Press 1992
10 http://www.puzzlemaker.com

A language reference resources
B ideas for planning lessons
C resources for teachers and learners producing their own materials
D materials for very young learners

## REFLECTION

1 What were the reference resources you used when you were studying English? Do they still help you?
2 What are the reference resources you use most often when preparing lessons? In what ways do they help you?
3 If you had to go and teach in a place with very few resources, which three reference books would you take with you?

## DISCOVERY ACTIVITIES

1 In your TKT portfolio, keep a record of the reference resources you use. Make notes of the source (title and author, website address, etc.), the lesson(s) you taught and any comments on the advantages or disadvantages of the resource.

2 Carry out an informal survey amongst your colleagues to find out what are the most popular and useful reference resources for the age(s) and level(s) of learners you teach. Keep a record of the results of your survey in your portfolio.

3 For some good advice on using reference resources for finding information about language, have a look at Chapter 12 of *The Practice of English Language Teaching* (third edition) by Jeremy Harmer, Pearson Education Ltd 2001.

4 For ideas on building up your own library of resources, look at Unit 12 ('Building a Resource Bank') of *LanguageAssistant* by Clare Lavery, downloadable free from: http://www.britishcouncil.org/languageassistant-manual.htm

5 Two very useful websites with large numbers of links to other sites with lesson plans, games, ideas about teaching and many other resources are: http://iteslj.org/links and http://www.eastment.com

**TKT practice task** *(See page 176 for answers)*

For questions 1–7, match the teachers' descriptions with the reference resources listed **A–H**.
There is one extra option which you do not need to use.

**Reference resources**

> A a language awareness book for teachers
> B a book to help teachers use one kind of resource
> C a teachers' magazine on the Internet
> D a picture dictionary
> E a learner's grammar book
> F a monolingual dictionary
> G a book about interference from different first languages
> H a bilingual dictionary

**Teachers' descriptions**

1 Sometimes I just need to check what a word means in my own language.
2 If you teach beginners all the time, it's good to have a book that helps you keep up your own language level.
3 I want my learners to read English definitions of English words.
4 It gives me information about rules and usage, written in language I can use in the classroom, and there are exercises for learners, too.
5 My school has just got some new computers, and this book gives me the ideas I need about how to use them.
6 My young learners find it easier to remember new words if they can see what things look like.
7 It has articles by teachers, lesson plans and worksheets you can print out and lots of useful links.

# Unit 23    Selection and use of coursebook materials

## How do we select and use coursebook materials?

Coursebook materials are all the materials in a coursebook package that we use in the classroom to **present** and practise language, and to develop learners' language **skills**.

A coursebook package usually includes a student's book, a **teacher's book** and audio and/or video recordings. The teacher's book often includes the **tapescript** (i.e. the words learners hear) of these recordings. Often there is also a **workbook** or **activity book** (a book with extra practice material), and there may also be a CD-ROM or extra material on a website.

Teachers often base their selection of teaching materials (coursebook or **supplementary**) on a 'needs analysis', i.e. a study of learners' level, language needs and interests, using questionnaires, interviews or **diagnostic tests**. This information helps to build up a **class profile** (a description of all the learners in the class) and shows what they have in common and how they differ from each other. The teacher's task is then to select the material that best matches this profile.

## Key concepts

What questions should we ask when selecting teaching materials?

We may not be able to choose our coursebook, but we can still make choices about what materials in it to use. Decisions about whether – and how – to use the coursebook or part of it will depend on the answers to a number of questions:

- Is the material visually attractive? Is it visually clear (e.g. using different colours, different fonts, headings, etc.)? Does the visual material help learners to understand context and meaning?
- Is it well organised? Can you and your learners follow the 'logic' of the material and find your way around the page or the unit quickly and easily?
- Is it culturally appropriate? Will the **context**(s) be familiar to learners?
- Is it suitable for your learners' age and their needs and interests?
- Will the topics be motivating to suit the age, gender, experience and personal interests of your learners?
- Is it at the right level? Does it provide a clear enough context and/or explanations for learners to understand new language?
- Does it give learners enough opportunities to use the language?

If the answer to any of these questions is 'No', then we have two choices:

- to replace the coursebook material with materials with the same focus/aim from another book or resource, such as a teachers' website or supplementary materials
- to **adapt** the coursebook material, i.e. change it in some way to make it suitable for our learners.

There are a number of ways to adapt material that is not suitable for a particular teaching situation. Here are some ideas:

| Strategies | Problems | Possible solutions |
|---|---|---|
| Extending material | • The **task** or exercise is too short.<br>• The learners need more practice. | • Write extra items, following the same pattern. |
| Shortening material | • The task or exercise is too long.<br>• The learners don't need so much practice. | • Use as much as you need, but do not feel you have to use it all.<br>• Give different parts of the text or task to different learners. |
| Changing the form of tasks | • The task doesn't suit the learners' learning style.<br>• You want a change of pace.<br>• The coursebook often repeats the same kind of task. | • Change the **interaction pattern**, e.g. use a matching task as a **mingling** activity (i.e. one in which learners move around the class, in this case to find their partners). |
| Changing the level of the material | • The texts or tasks are too easy or too difficult. | • Make material more challenging, e.g. learners try to answer comprehension questions *before* reading.<br>• Make material less challenging, e.g. break up a long text into shorter sections. |
| Reordering material | • The activities in the units in the book always follow the same **sequence**.<br>• The learners need to learn or practise things in a different order. | • Change the order of the material, e.g. ask learners to cover up a page or part of a page, so that they focus on what you want them to do first. |
| Making use of all the resources in the book | • There is not enough practice material in a particular unit.<br>• The learners need to revise particular items.<br>• You want to preview material in a future unit. | • Use extra material from the book: grammar summaries, word lists, lists of irregular verbs, etc.<br>• Give whole-book tasks, e.g. searching through the book for texts, pictures, language examples. |

# Key concepts and the language teaching classroom

- There may be good reasons for leaving out part of a unit, or even a whole unit, but remember that the coursebook is one of the main sources of learning (and revision) for our learners. So they may find it confusing if we do this too often.
- The coursebook will normally provide the main content for a lesson, while material that needs to be more **personalised** for the learners will probably come from the teacher (or from the learners themselves). When planning lessons, think about what the coursebook gives you, and what you need to add. For example:

| Coursebook provides: | Teacher can provide additional: |
|---|---|
| • situation/context | • **warmer** |
| • pictures | • instructions |
| • **dialogues** (conversations between two people) and texts | • **role-play** |
| • tasks and exercises | • homework tasks |

- If we plan to reorder the material in the coursebook, we must make sure that this is possible, i.e. that a task/exercise does not depend on a previous one.
- We can change the order of activities in the coursebook in order to introduce **variety** in one of the following areas: **pace**, interaction pattern, sequence of skills practice, level of difficulty, content, mood, etc.
- We should think about how to make material more attractive and interesting for learners and how to bring material 'off the page', e.g. using mime, pictures, **realia** (real objects such as clothes or food), etc.

> See Units 13 and 14 for learner characteristics and needs, Unit 24 for the selection and use of supplementary materials and Unit 25 for the selection and use of aids.

## FOLLOW-UP ACTIVITIES (See page 174 for answers)

1 Select a unit from your coursebook that you haven't used yet and answer the questions on page 110.
2 In what way(s) will you need to adapt the material? Make notes in your TKT portfolio.

## REFLECTION

Think about these comments from teachers. Which do you agree with and why?
1 I plan my lessons to respond to my learners' needs, so I never use a coursebook.
2 I always plan my lessons following the suggestions in the teacher's book.
3 I use all the material in every unit in the order given in the book.
4 I use a coursebook, but I change most of it so that learners don't get bored.
5 I've got a good coursebook and I haven't got time to adapt any of it.

## DISCOVERY ACTIVITIES

1 If you have colleagues who have used the same coursebook, find out from them what worked well in their classes, what was less successful and what they had to change. If you are the first teacher in your school to use the book, keep a 'coursebook diary' in your TKT portfolio, and make notes about its advantages and disadvantages.

2 For further ideas on using coursebooks, have a look at Chapter 4 of *Teaching Practice Handbook* (second edition) by Roger Gower, Diane Phillips and Steve Walters, Macmillan 1995 and Chapter 5, Part 2 of *Planning Lessons and Courses* by Tessa Woodward, Cambridge University Press 2001. For ideas on using other materials, look at Chapter 3, Section 1 of *Learning Teaching* by Jim Scrivener (2nd edition, Macmillan 2005) and Module 13, Units One, Two and Three of *A Course in Language Teaching* by Penny Ur, Cambridge University Press 1996.

3 You can find some very interesting articles, discussion and resources on teaching without a coursebook at http://www.teaching-unplugged.com

**TKT practice task** *(See page 176 for answers)*

For questions 1-7, match the coursebook instructions with the activity aims listed **A-H**. There is one extra option which you do not need to use.

### Activity aims

A accurate use of a specific structure
B finding collocations
C reading for gist
D oral fluency practice
E finding connections in a text
F listening for detailed information
G writing a short story
H listening for gist

### Coursebook instructions

1 Look quickly through the text and choose the picture that matches the situation.
2 Complete the sentences below using one of the following modal verbs.
3 Play the cassette again and answer the true/false questions.
4 Underline all the pronouns and draw arrows to show the nouns they refer to.
5 Choose the words that go together.
6 In groups of three, discuss the problem and decide on the best solution.
7 Look at the photographs and decide who you think is speaking.

# Unit 24   Selection and use of supplementary materials and activities

## ◼ How do we select and use supplementary materials and activities?

**Supplementary materials** are books and other materials we can use in addition to the coursebook. They include **skills** development materials, grammar, vocabulary and phonology practice materials, collections of **communicative activities** and teacher's **resource** materials. Supplementary materials may also come from **authentic** sources (e.g. newspaper and magazine articles, video, etc.). Some coursebook packages include supplementary materials and activities specially designed to fit the coursebook **syllabus**, and there are also many websites where you can download supplementary materials. We select supplementary materials and activities first by recognising that we need something more than (or different from) the material in the coursebook, and then by knowing where to find the most appropriate kinds of material.

## ◼ Key concepts

Make a list of all the reasons you can think of for using supplementary materials and activities. What are the advantages and disadvantages of using the supplementary materials in the box below?

---

- a class library of **graded readers** (storybooks that use simple language)
- skills practice books
- teacher's resource books
- websites
- videos
- language practice books (grammar/vocabulary/phonology)
- electronic materials (CD-ROMs, computer programs)
- games

---

There are various reasons why we might want to use supplementary materials and activities. Some of the main reasons are as follows:

- to replace unsuitable material in the coursebook
- to fill gaps in the coursebook
- to provide suitable material for learners' particular needs and interests
- to give learners extra language or skills practice
- to add variety to our teaching.

Coursebooks are organised according to a syllabus, and they are often carefully **graded** (i.e. **grammatical structures**, vocabulary, skills, etc. are presented in a helpful **sequence** for learning), so that learners' knowledge of the language builds up step by step through the book. Supplementary materials and activities can provide **variety** in lessons and useful extra practice, but it is important to make sure that they fit into the learners' programme, are suitable for the class and match the **aims** for particular lessons. Here are some of the possible advantages and disadvantages of different kinds of supplementary materials:

| | Possible advantages | Possible disadvantages |
|---|---|---|
| Class library of readers | • encourages **extensive reading**<br>• gives learners confidence | • language sometimes too simple<br>• may not be challenging |
| Skills practice books | • focus on individual skills | • may not fit coursebook |
| Teacher's resource books | • new ideas for lessons | • may not suit lesson aims |
| Websites | • variety of lesson plans, teaching materials, other resources | • sometimes difficult to find the right material for the learners |
| Video | • provides visual **context**<br>• source of cultural information<br>• shows body language | • equipment may not always be available<br>• language may not be graded |
| Language practice books | • extra practice<br>• learners can work alone without teacher's help | • repetitive exercises<br>• little or no context |
| Electronic materials | • **motivation**<br>• familiar technology for learners | • difficult for teacher to control how learners are working<br>• little or no human **feedback** |
| Games | • enjoyment<br>• language practice | • may not be suitable for older learners |

# Key concepts and the language teaching classroom

*Selection of supplementary materials and activities*

- Get to know what supplementary materials are available in your school. Use a questionnaire or interviews for needs analysis (see page 110) at the beginning of the course to find out what you will want to add to the coursebook when you are planning your **scheme of work**.
- Supplementary language practice materials are not always accompanied by teacher's books, and the aims of activities may not be clear. When selecting material, therefore, you need to think about exactly how it will replace or improve on material in your coursebook.
- It may be useful to use authentic material (which is not designed for a particular level), in order to give learners the experience of working with more challenging texts and **tasks**.
- The activities in materials designed to develop individual skills often include the use of other skills, e.g. learners need to read a text before they carry out a listening task, or to do some writing as a follow-up activity after a speaking activity. When selecting materials and activities, think carefully about all the skills that are required.
- Many publishers produce materials for practising separate language skills at different levels. Teacher's resource books, too, usually list tasks and activities according to level. Before deciding to use these materials, however, you should check how appropriate the level is for your learners. Think about the language they will need to understand or to produce.

*Use of supplementary materials and activities*

- Learners get used to the methodology in their coursebook. If you are using supplementary materials with very different **procedures**, you may need to give special attention to instructions.
- You can **adapt** many supplementary materials for use with classes at different levels. The texts used in these materials may not be graded, but you can grade the activities by making the learners' tasks more or less challenging.
- Games and extra communicative activities can provide variety and make learning fun. But you need to think about your reasons for using them, so that your lesson still has a clear purpose. Older learners may want to know why they are doing these activities.

See Unit 22 for consulting reference resources and Unit 23 for the selection and use of coursebook materials.

**FOLLOW-UP ACTIVITY** *(See page 174 for answers)*

Here are ten sets of instructions for the kinds of activities you might find in a book of supplementary materials.  For each one, decide:
– what level(s) it is suitable for (i.e. elementary, intermediate, advanced)
– what you think the aims are
– what materials (if any) the teacher needs to prepare
– if it focuses on particular language.

1  In pairs, compare your list of ideas for staying healthy. Then agree on the six most useful ideas. Next, get together with another pair and decide on a group list of the six best ideas. Put these ideas in order according to their usefulness.

2  Describe the picture to your partner so that s/he can draw it. When you have finished, compare your pictures and discuss the reasons for any differences.

3  Send one member of your group outside the classroom to read the next sentence. He or she must remember the sentence without writing it down, then come back and dictate the sentence to the group.

4  Use your dictionary to find as much information as you can about your word. Discuss with the other students in your group how the meanings of your words are connected and then explain the connections to the class.

5  Decide which stories are true and which are false. Then choose one to tell to the rest of the class for them to make the same decision.

6  Read the definition to the class for them to guess the word.

7  Listen to the words on the recording and check whether you have underlined the correct syllables.

8  Correct the text so that it matches the information in the picture.

9  Write the next part of the story on the computer. When you have finished, move to the next computer and continue the story you see on the screen.

10  Go to the blackboard and rub out one word in the sentence, so that the words that are left on the board still form a correct sentence.

## REFLECTION

Think about these comments from teachers. Which do you agree with and why?

1 There's more than enough material in my coursebook. I don't have time to use supplementary materials.

2 My students get bored with the same book in every lesson, so I use supplementary materials as often as I can.

3 I'd like to use supplementary materials more often, but I find it difficult to fit them into my syllabus.

## DISCOVERY ACTIVITIES

1 Keep a record of the supplementary materials you use during one week's teaching. Make notes on the reasons for using the material, how it worked and what changes you would make if you used it again. Put your notes in your TKT portfolio.

2 Choose two or three supplementary activities you have used recently. Make notes on the changes you would need to make to use the material at different levels.

3 For ideas on using – and making – supplementary materials, have a look at Module 13, Units Four and Five of *A Course in Language Teaching* by Penny Ur, Cambridge University Press 1996, Chapter 16, Sections 2–4 and 8–9 of *Learning Teaching* by Jim Scrivener (2nd edition, Macmillan 2005) and Chapter 4 of *Teaching Practice Handbook* (second edition) by Roger Gower, Diane Phillips and Steve Walters, Macmillan 1995.

4 You can find more ideas for using supplementary materials at Dave's ESL Café http://www.eslcafe.com/ideas/index.html and a very useful list of links to other websites where you can find supplementary materials at http://www.eastment.com/links.html

**TKT practice task** *(See page 176 for answers)*

For questions 1-7, choose which book listed **A-G** could help a teacher who made the following comments.

There is one extra option which you do not need to use.

## Books

A *The Internet and the Language Classroom* Gavin Dudeney, Cambridge University Press

B *Developing Listening Skills* Shelagh Rixon, Prentice Hall

C *Sounds Like This* Katie Kitching, Belair Publications Ltd

D *Simple Speaking Activities* Jill Hadfield and Charles Hadfield, Oxford University Press

E *Elementary Language Practice* Michael Vince, Macmillan

F *Literature in the Language Classroom* Joanne Collie and Stephen Slater, Cambridge University Press

G *Words in Their Places: Graded Cloze Texts and Comprehension Exercises* Lynn Hutchinson, Hodder Arnold

### Teacher's comments

1 I've been teaching for a long time, but I really need some fresh ideas for teaching grammar to low-level learners.

2 I'm not sure how to use websites for teaching English.

3 I'm looking for activities to help my teenage elementary learners develop their fluency, but I haven't got time to do a lot of extra preparation.

4 I'm interested in using poems and short stories in my language classes.

5 I want a book that explains pronunciation and gives me some ideas about how to teach it.

6 My learners need lots of extra tasks for reading practice, but I haven't got time to search for supplementary materials at the right level.

# Unit 25   Selection and use of teaching aids

## How do we select and use teaching aids?

**Teaching aids** are the **resources** and equipment available to us in the classroom, as well as the resources we can bring into the classroom. They include cassette recorders, CD players, video recorders and **overhead projectors** (i.e. equipment with a light in it that can make images appear larger on a screen), **visual aids** (pictures that can help learners understand), **realia** and the teacher himself/herself! We select and use aids by thinking carefully about the **main aims** and the **subsidiary aims** of a lesson, and then choosing the most appropriate ones.

## Key concepts

Look at the following list of classroom equipment. What other teaching purposes can you think of for each item?

| Classroom equipment | Main teaching purpose |
|---|---|
| blackboard/whiteboard | writing up planned vocabulary, grammar examples and explanations |
| overhead projector (OHP) | displaying prepared exercises on **transparencies** (plastic sheets) |
| cassette recorder/CD player | listening practice |
| video recorder | listening practice with added visual information |
| computer | grammar exercises |
| **language laboratory** (i.e. a room where learners can listen to recordings and record themselves) | grammar drills |

All of these aids can be used for many different purposes. Some examples of these purposes are on the next page.

| Blackboard/whiteboard | Video recorder |
|---|---|
| • writing words and ideas that come up during the lesson<br>• drawing or displaying pictures<br>• building up ideas in diagrams, word maps, etc.<br>• for learners to write answers<br>• for whole-class compositions | • for **information gap** tasks (with one learner viewing and one just listening)<br>• viewing without sound and guessing the language<br>• pausing and **predicting** the language (i.e. saying what you think is coming next)<br>• with a camera, filming learners' performance |
| Overhead projector | Computer |
| • displaying results of group work<br>• building up information by putting one transparency on top of another<br>• covering up or gradually uncovering parts of the transparency<br>• displaying pictures and diagrams on photocopiable transparencies | • narrative building with a word processor<br>• supplementary materials for coursebooks<br>• online language tests<br>• using online dictionaries<br>• using CD-ROMs<br>• email exchanges<br>• online communication (chatting)<br>• online newspapers and magazines<br>• project work using the Internet |
| Cassette recorder/CD player | Language laboratory |
| • **presenting** new language in **dialogues** and stories<br>• giving models for pronunciation practice<br>• recording learners' oral performance<br>• listening for pleasure | • pronunciation practice<br>• **extensive listening**<br>• **monitoring** and giving **feedback** to individual learners<br>• developing speaking **skills** |

Other aids are: realia, **flashcards** (cards small enough to hold up one after another, with simple drawings or single words or phrases on them), **puppets** (models of people or animals that you can move by putting your hand inside them), **charts** (diagrams that show information) and the teacher.

What different uses can you think of for these aids?

Here are some of the most important uses:

*Realia*

Real objects that we can easily bring into the classroom can be used to teach vocabulary, as prompts for practising **grammatical structures** or for building dialogues and narratives, for games and quizzes. Realia also include real texts, such as menus, timetables, leaflets, etc.

*Flashcards*
Like realia, flashcards can be used for teaching individual words or as prompts for practising grammatical structures.

*Puppets*
Puppets are an excellent resource for teaching young learners. For example, we can introduce new language in dialogues between pairs of puppets (or between one puppet and the teacher). Children can also make their own simple puppets.

*Charts*
We can use posters and **wallcharts** (drawings or graphs that can be put on the wall of a classroom) to display larger, more detailed pictures, or a series of pictures telling a story or showing related objects in a **lexical set**. A **phonemic chart** shows the **phonemic symbols** and the positions in the mouth where the different sounds are made. The teacher can point at the symbols to prompt learners to correct their pronunciation. We can also use charts to display diagrams, prepared drawings and tables of irregular **verbs**, or to build up a class dictionary.

*The teacher*
The teacher can use hand **gestures**, **facial expressions** and **mime** (actions which express meaning without words) to **elicit** vocabulary items, clarify meaning and create **context**. We can also build up a set of signals, such as finger correction, which learners recognise as prompts to correct their own mistakes.

## Key concepts and the language teaching classroom

- It is a good idea to divide the blackboard or whiteboard into different sections for different purposes, as in this example:

| Reference material (e.g. key **lexis**, model sentences, grammar rules, etc.) | Lesson materials (e.g. pictures, key grammatical structures, dialogues, etc.) at different stages of the lesson | Vocabulary notepad for noting all new words |
|---|---|---|

You can include diagrams like this in your lesson plan for different stages of the lesson.

- Aids that you can prepare in advance, like charts, flashcards and transparencies for the overhead projector, will help you to make sure that lesson **procedures** match your aims. Another advantage is that you can save such aids and reuse them in future lessons.
- Make sure that you check any equipment before the lesson. Use the counters on cassette recorders and video recorders to make a note of where recordings begin, so that you can find the place easily when you rewind.
- If you use computers or the language laboratory, advance preparation is essential. You need to plan all your instructions very carefully, as well as the **sequence** of activities for the lesson.

*See Unit 23 for the selection and use of teaching materials and Unit 24 for the selection and use of supplementary materials.*

## FOLLOW-UP ACTIVITY *(See page 174 for answers)*

Which aids do you think these teachers are talking about?

1  I can prepare lots of material in advance, and I don't have to make lots of photocopies.
2  It gives me a chance to listen to all the learners individually.
3  Whenever I travel abroad, I collect all kinds of things to use in class.
4  I use them as prompts for a dialogue with the whole class, then give them out to pairs so they can practise.
5  I always use one part of it as a kind of notebook for new words.
6  It gives learners the most realistic kind of listening practice.
7  This helps with tests, grammar and vocabulary exercises, dictionary work, research – just about everything.

## REFLECTION

1  Think about the aids you use most often. What learner characteristics make some aids more successful than others in different classes?
2  What are the advantages and disadvantages of using technical equipment in the classroom? (For example, think about planning, motivation and technical problems.)
3  Which aids are the most motivating for your learners? (For example, younger learners may learn best through playing games, while teenagers may enjoy working with computers.)

## DISCOVERY ACTIVITIES

1  In your TKT portfolio, keep a record of the aids that you use. Make notes in a grid like the one below of the aids you use, the lesson aims, comments on how successful they have been and any changes you might need to make in future.

| Aids used | Lesson aims | Comments | Changes for future lessons |
|-----------|-------------|----------|----------------------------|
|           |             |          |                            |

2  If you always use the same aids for a particular teaching purpose (e.g. always using a recorded dialogue or a reading text to introduce a new grammatical structure), try doing it differently, and make notes in your portfolio about the advantages and disadvantages of using these different techniques.
3  For some very useful ideas on the use of aids, have a look at Chapter 10 of *The Practice of English Language Teaching* (third edition) by Jeremy Harmer, Pearson Education Ltd 2001, Chapter 3 of *Teaching Practice Handbook* (second edition) by Roger Gower, Diane Phillips and Steve Walters, Macmillan 1995 and Chapter 10 of *Children Learning English* by Jayne Moon, Macmillan 2000.
4  You can also find some interesting articles on using aids on this website: http://www.teachingenglish.org.uk/think/resources.shtml
5  Use the *TKT Glossary* to find the meaning of these terms for aids: *crossword puzzle, flipchart, leaflet, video clip*. Ask colleagues what they have used them for.

........................................................................................................

**TKT practice task** *(See page 176 for answers)*

For questions 1-7, match the teaching purposes with the aids listed **A-H**.
There is one extra option which you do not need to use.

_____

### Aids

> **A** realia
> **B** OHP
> **C** puppets
> **D** video
> **E** self-access centre
> **F** computer
> **G** phonemic chart
> **H** blackboard/whiteboard

### Teaching purposes

1  to show learners pictures or answers to tasks prepared before the lesson
2  to remind learners about pronunciation
3  for learners to work by themselves and improve their performance
4  to give learners listening practice with visual context
5  to note down new vocabulary items throughout the lesson
6  to bring small things from the world outside into the classroom
7  to ask learners to find information for project work independently

........................................................................................................

*A sample answer sheet is on page 168.*

For questions **1-8**, match the lesson aims with the learner group profiles listed **A-I**.

Mark the correct letter (**A-I**) on your answer sheet.

There is one extra option which you do not need to use.

### Lesson aims

1. to practise answering enquiries on the telephone
2. to practise note-taking skills
3. to provide learners with basic vocabulary for tourism
4. to develop strategies for planning and doing timed essays
5. to practise giving clear explanations and instructions
6. to revise spelling and basic sentence patterns
7. to diagnose learners' language needs
8. to make connections with other school subjects

### Learner group profiles

A    a group of office workers

B    a class of advanced learners who have to take a test of writing

C    a large class of mixed-level 13-year-olds in a secondary school

D    a small group of adults planning a holiday in Britain

E    a class of beginners aged four

F    a new group of learners whose level is not known to the teacher

G    a group of primary teachers preparing for an oral test

H    an individual learner who has difficulties with writing in English

I    a group of university students who need English to listen to lectures

For questions **9-18**, match the teacher's instructions with the aims for different lesson stages listed **A-F**.

Mark the correct letter (**A-F**) on your answer sheet.

You need to use some options more than once.

Aims

| | |
|---|---|
| A | reading for gist |
| B | identifying features of connected speech |
| C | listening for gist |
| D | listening for specific information |
| E | grouping vocabulary according to meaning |
| F | focusing on structures |

Teacher's instructions

**9** Find all the words and phrases you can think of which are connected with keeping fit.

**10** Listen to the story to get a general idea of what it is about.

**11** With your partner, read the words and decide which one is different from the others, and why.

**12** Listen again and mark the correct route on the map.

**13** Listen to the pairs of sentences and say if they are stressed on the same or a different word.

**14** Listen carefully, and mark each sentence with an arrow going up or down.

**15** Choose the past simple or the present perfect to complete the sentences.

**16** Underline all the examples of the passive in the text and say why the writer chooses this form.

**17** When you have finished the story, decide on the best title for it.

**18** Decide which words go together in lexical sets.

For questions **19-28**, match the teacher's notes with the lesson plan headings **A-E**.

Mark the correct letter (**A-E**) on your answer sheet.

You need to use some options more than once.

**Lesson plan headings**

| | |
|---|---|
| A | Timetable fit |
| B | Main or subsidiary aim(s) |
| C | Personal aims |
| D | Assumptions |
| E | Procedures |

**Teacher's notes**

| 19 | to practise talking about daily or weekly routines, e.g. in the context of journeys to school, hobbies, sports activities |
|---|---|
| 20 | learners will remember the form of the present simple |
| 21 | learners listen to a recording of someone talking about her morning routine and fill in the information on a diary page |
| 22 | learners carry out a class survey |
| 23 | to try to speak louder |
| 24 | put a simple chart on the board to remind learners of differences between the adverbs |
| 25 | learners will probably not remember the different meanings of the adverbs |
| 26 | to use different forms of encouragement when learners give correct answers |
| 27 | the first in a sequence of grammar revision lessons |
| 28 | to revise the present simple; to revise adverbs (e.g. *sometimes*, *usually*, *always*) |

For questions **29-34**, read the stages of the lesson plan about giving warnings and advice and fill in the missing stages from the options listed **A-F**.

Mark the correct letter (**A-F**) on your answer sheet.

| | |
|---|---|
| A | Individually, learners answer true/false questions to check comprehension. |
| B | Learners underline examples of warnings and advice in the text. |
| C | Learners display their posters on the classroom wall. |
| D | Ask learners to talk in groups about their holiday experiences. |
| E | Individually, learners write different sections of the poster. |
| F | In pairs, learners guess the content of a text about holidays from the headlines. |

| |
|---|
| Aims: to practise giving warnings and advice; to develop writing skills |
| • Warmer: Find your partner – students mingle to find partners with matching sentence halves. |
| 29 ............................................ |
| • In pairs, students brainstorm vocabulary connected with holidays. |
| 30 ............................................ |
| • Individually, students read the text to check their predictions. |
| 31 ............................................ |
| • In pairs, students check their answers and report back to the class on any disagreements. |
| 32 ............................................ |
| • In groups, students brainstorm ideas for a poster. |
| 33 ............................................ |
| • Students correct and make suggestions for improving each other's writing |
| 34 ............................................ |

For questions **35-40**, match the instructions with the assessment focuses listed **A, B** or **C**.

Mark the correct letter (**A, B** or **C**) on your answer sheet.

### Assessment focuses

| | |
|---|---|
| A | language items |
| B | oral skills |
| C | writing skills |

### Instructions

**35** Share the information with the other members of your group, and decide which of these people you think should get the job.

**36** Describe your picture to your partner and find out what your pictures have in common.

**37** Complete each sentence with a word from the box.

**38** Fill in the form with your personal information.

**39** Order these ideas to make a plan for a composition.

**40** Match the words in the left-hand column with the definitions in the right-hand column.

For questions **41-48**, read the following dictionary entry. Match the extracts from the dictionary entry with the information they provide, listed **A-I**.

Mark the correct letter (**A-I**) on your answer sheet.

There is one extra option which you do not need to use.

**Dictionary entry**

> **performance** /pəˈfɔːmənts/ (US) /pɚˈfɔːr-/ *noun* [C] **1** the action of entertaining other people
> by dancing, singing, acting or playing music: *a performance of Arthur Miller's play 'The
> Crucible'* o *She gave a superb performance as Lady Macbeth.* **2** MAINLY UK INFORMAL **a
> performance** an action or behaviour that involves a lot of attention to detail or to small matters
> that are not important: *Cleaning the oven is such a performance.* o *What a performance!
> Please stop shouting!* **3 repeat performance** when an event or a situation happens again: *The
> police hope to avoid a repeat performance of last year, when the festivities turned into rioting.*

(from the *Cambridge Advanced Learner's Dictionary*)

| Extracts from the dictionary entry | Information |
|---|---|
| **41** /pəˈfɔːmənts/ | A American English |
| **42** (US) | B noun–noun collocation |
| **43** *noun* | C definition |
| **44** [C] | D part of speech |
| **45** *the action of entertaining other people by dancing, singing, acting or playing music* | E pronunciation |
| **46** *gave ... performance* | F old word |
| **47** INFORMAL | G countable noun |
| **48** **repeat performance** | H register |
| | I verb–noun collocation |

For questions **49-55**, match the teachers' statements with the reference resources listed **A-H**.

Mark the correct letter (**A-H**) on your answer sheet.

There is one extra option which you do not need to use.

**Reference resources**

| | |
|---|---|
| A | advanced learner's grammar |
| B | picture dictionary |
| C | language awareness book for teachers |
| D | CD-ROM with pronunciation activities |
| E | elementary grammar practice book |
| F | dictionary of collocations |
| G | dictionary of language and culture |
| H | practice book accompanying a coursebook |

**Teachers' statements**

**49** I often find it difficult to know which words go together.

**50** I'd like to find a book that helps me to understand and use English better.

**51** I'm looking for ways of explaining new structures to my class of beginners.

**52** I teach a lot of different classes, so I can't prepare homework exercises for all my learners.

**53** I need a way of helping my young learners develop their vocabulary.

**54** My advanced learners often want to know about people, places and events in newspapers and films.

**55** My higher-level learners sometimes ask me questions about language that I find very difficult to answer.

For questions **56-65**, match the comments from teachers about their coursebooks with the appropriate strategies for adapting materials listed **A-D**.

Mark the correct letter (**A-D**) on your answer sheet.

You need to use some options more than once.

### Strategies

| | |
|---|---|
| **A** | Shorten the material. |
| **B** | Reorder the material. |
| **C** | Change the level of the material. |
| **D** | Change the form of the tasks. |

### Comments from teachers

56 All the units in the book begin with pairwork, but my learners are not very confident about speaking.

57 The exercises in the book are quite good, but they're a bit too simple.

58 All the reading tasks in the book are very similar – my learners need more variety.

59 The reading tasks in my book don't challenge my young learners enough.

60 Some of the exercises in the book are too difficult for my class.

61 The revision exercises in the book come at the end of every unit, but I like to begin my lessons with some quick revision.

62 The mingling activities make my class too excited so I do them as group work instead.

63 Every unit sets the scene with questions about a picture, but I sometimes like to use a brainstorming activity about the picture instead.

64 Some of my learners are making good progress and find the exercises too easy.

65 My young learners can't concentrate on such long listening passages.

For questions **66-75**, match the supplementary materials with the teaching aims listed **A-G**.

Mark the correct letter (**A-G**) on your answer sheet.

You need to use some options more than once.

---

**Supplementary materials**

66 grammar book with team games and group activities

67 class library of graded readers

68 audio cassettes with short examples of different kinds of English

69 computer program with multiple-choice reading tests and answers

70 website for short stories

71 supplementary writing skills book

72 workbook with gap-fill and multiple-choice grammar exercises

73 flashcards with pictures of objects and their names

74 supplementary vocabulary book with photocopiable worksheets

75 teacher's resource book with lots of short fun activities

**Teaching aims**

A    encouraging extensive reading

B    providing resources for self-assessment

C    providing ideas for warmers

D    developing the subskills of organising, planning and accuracy

E    developing lexical knowledge

F    improving learners' accuracy

G    giving learners the opportunity to hear a variety of accents

For questions **76-80**, match the classroom aids with the classroom activities listed **A-F**.

Mark the correct letter (**A-F**) on your answer sheet.

There is one extra option which you do not need to use.

| Classroom aids | Classroom activities |
|---|---|
| 76 overhead projector | A drafting and redrafting |
| 77 computer | B mingling to complete a survey |
| 78 role cards | C learning the meaning of new vocabulary items |
| 79 cassette recorder | D guessing how a conversation will continue |
| 80 flashcards | E less controlled speaking practice |
| | F showing pictures on coloured transparencies |

# Managing the teaching and learning process

**Part 1** Teachers' and learners' language in the classroom

**Unit 26** Using language appropriately for a range of classroom functions

■ How do we use language appropriately for a range of classroom functions?

Using language appropriately means we use language in the classroom which best suits the learners and the situation. Classroom functions are the purposes for which teachers and learners use language in the classroom. For teachers, these purposes include, for example, to manage activities and learning, to explain learning points and to move smoothly from one stage of a lesson to the next.

■ Key concepts

What are some common classroom functions used by the teacher?

Here are some classroom functions that are often used by the teacher:

   **Instructing**. We give instructions (i.e. tell learners what to do) at different stages of the lesson, for example at the beginning of an activity. The language of instructions is often the imperative, particularly for young learners and for beginners, as in 'Open your books at page 12'. For learners at higher levels, we might use other language forms, for example: 'For this activity, you're going to work in pairs.'

   Explaining. We might explain to learners how to do an activity, how to organise a project they are doing, the meaning of vocabulary or why a correction is needed. For example, when explaining about project work we might say: 'We'll put the project work on the walls so you need to make sure that everything is easy to read and that it looks wonderful.'

   **Narrating**. Narrating is telling a story or talking about something that has happened. In the primary classroom we often tell stories to learners. In secondary and adult classrooms we may tell stories too, but we might more often talk about past experiences and things that have happened in our lives.

   **Eliciting**. Eliciting is when we get information from our learners rather than giving it to them. This information can be about topics or language. For example, we can show learners a picture and ask 'What can you see in the picture?' We can also ask learners to give us general information, e.g. what a certain animal eats.

**Prompting** learners. Prompting is when we say something to help learners think of ideas, or to remember a word or phrase by giving them part of it. For example, we could say to learners at the start of a storytelling activity 'You could start the story with this picture', or if a learner can't remember a word, we could help them with the first sound, such as *com* for *competition*.

Correcting. We can correct learners by using language to indicate where or how they have made a mistake.

Checking learning. We check learning all the time during our lessons, but we do this most often after we have **presented** new language, and at the end of a lesson to give us information for planning the next lesson(s). We can use **concept questions** to check learners' understanding, for example: 'Can anyone give me a sentence using this word?'

**Conveying** the **meaning** of new language. When we convey meaning we show the meaning of new words or structures. We can do this in a number of ways, such as bringing in **realia**, using **mime** or by asking concept questions. We may want to explain the meaning, to demonstrate it, or in some situations where the meaning is very difficult to explain in English, to translate it.

## Key concepts and the language teaching classroom

- The language we use in the classroom must be appropriate for the classroom function and for the level and age of the learners. For example, we should not use language that is too formal with primary learners or language that is too babyish with older learners.

- We need to **grade** our **language** to suit the language level and age of the learners. Grading language means choosing to use classroom language that is at or below the language level of the learners. For example, with beginners we use simple words and phrases, but with higher-level learners our language can be more complex. Grading means that our language is at the right level for the learners to understand.

- We need to sequence our language appropriately to provide learners with learning opportunities. **Sequencing** means using language in a logical order. This is particularly important for explanations and instructions, for example: 'Listen. Work with a partner.' rather than 'Work with a partner. Listen.'

- Learners can learn classroom language, just by hearing it again and again. So it is important to use the same classroom language for classroom functions at the early stages of learning, for example: 'Open your books and look at page ....' We can then build up these phrases to suit the learners' level and age.

- We need to think about the language we are going to use for different classroom functions and make sure the language we use is appropriate. Appropriate language will use the right degree of formality for the learners, be well graded and sequenced and clear. If we do not plan or think about the language we use, we might use the **L1**, or language which is too complex, which would not be helpful to learning.

*See Unit 4 for functions.*

## FOLLOW-UP ACTIVITIES *(See page 174 for answers)*

1  Look at the list of classroom functions in *Key concepts* above, and at the activities carried out by a teacher below. At which stage of a lesson might you use the different classroom functions? You will find that you can use more than one classroom function at each stage.

*Stages of a lesson*
A  Presenting new vocabulary
B  Telling the class a story and encouraging them to join in
C  Brainstorming ideas for a writing task with the whole class
D  Monitoring learners during a controlled practice activity
E  Giving feedback after a task

2  Read this teacher's instructions to children on how to make a rabbit (bunny) puppet. Which language form does the teacher use for each instruction and which conjunctions does she use to sequence the instructions?

> Now watch me first. Take the scissors and cut. Start with the bunny's head. OK, be careful. Cut round the head and now his big ears … his big ears that go flop, flop, flop. And up the ear and down again and round his head. Then, cut here round the bunny's face and round his shoulder and down round his body and now down to his feet.

(adapted from *English for Primary Teachers* by Mary Slattery and Jane Willis, Oxford University Press 2001)

## REFLECTION

Think about these comments from teachers. Which do you agree with and why?
1  I don't need to plan the language I use for giving instructions. I just think of what to say at the time and I know when my learners understand.
2  My learners speak the same L1 as I do. So it's much better to use the mother tongue for setting up activities and checking understanding.
3  I have a collection of different phrases that I use for managing my classes. I choose from these phrases when I am planning my lessons. I teach different levels, but I find I can use the same language for each level.

## DISCOVERY ACTIVITIES

1  For useful examples of different classroom functions and language, have a look at Chapter 5 of *Learning Teaching* by Jim Scrivener (2nd edition, Macmillan 2005).
2  Look through your next lesson plan and try and match the different classroom functions you have read about in this unit with the stages of your lesson.
3  Try writing a set of instructions for an activity for your learners. You can choose from activities at http://www.smic.be/smic5022/teacherhandouts.htm
4  Use the *TKT Glossary* or a dictionary to find the meaning of these terms for classroom functions: *define, model, nominate*.

## TKT practice task *(See page 176 for answers)*

For questions 1-5, look at the following situations and three possible things a teacher could say. Choose the most appropriate option **A, B or C**.

1 In a class of primary children of 9–10 years of age, the learners are finishing a pairwork task. The teacher wants to check the answers with the class.
   A What's the answer to number 1? Hands up, please.
   B Can any of you possibly tell me what you think might be the answer for the first question?
   C Answer?

2 In a class of teenagers in their second year of English, the teacher has just presented a new grammatical structure and wants to check that the learners understand the meaning.
   A Does everyone understand?
   B Who can give me an example sentence?
   C Please explain the meaning.

3 A group of businessmen are doing a discussion activity. The teacher notices a learner has made a mistake and says:
   A That's wrong.
   B A bad answer.
   C Is that quite right?

4 In a class of adult learners of mixed levels, the teacher is giving the first instruction for a complex group activity.
   A You all know what to do so you can start.
   B First, get into the groups you were in yesterday.
   C Here's the handout for the activity. You can start.

5 The teacher is telling a story to a class of very young primary learners who have only been learning English for one month.
   A Here is a little boy. Look. One day …
   B This is a story about a little boy who used to live in the city.
   C Stories are very important for you. They will help you learn new grammar.

# Unit 27  Identifying the functions of learners' language

## ▦ How do we identify the functions of learners' language?

The **functions** of learners' language are the purposes for which learners use language in the classroom. These purposes include taking part in tasks and activities, asking questions of the teacher, interacting with each other. Examples of the functions of learners' language are **asking for clarification** from the teacher or other learners, and checking information or understanding.

## ▦ Key concepts

Can you think of some common functions of learners' language?

Read through this description of a lesson. There are examples of learners' language functions for each **stage**.

| Learners' language functions | Teacher's and learners' actions |
|---|---|
| Greeting | The teacher enters the classroom and the learners say 'Good morning'. The teacher hands out a reading text and gives learners instructions for the reading task. |
| Asking for clarification | The learners check the instructions with the teacher by asking 'Can you explain that again please? What do we have to do?' |
| Checking information and understanding | The learners complete the reading task individually. The learners check their answers in pairs. They say, e.g. 'What answer do you have for number 4? I don't understand the meaning of this word. Do you know what it means?' The teacher checks the answers. |
| Saying goodbye | The lesson ends. The learners say 'Goodbye' to each other and to the teacher. |

## ▦ Key concepts and the language teaching classroom

- Learners need a range of classroom language so that they can **interact** appropriately with each other and with the teacher. The language that learners need for interacting with each other may sometimes be quite formal, and at other times more relaxed, depending on who is in the group. The language they need for interacting with the teacher is often neutral or more formal.

- Learners need to know special words and phrases for certain games and activities. For example, *It's my turn / It's your turn / I'm first / After you / I've won.*
- We need to teach our learners the language for a range of learners' classroom functions. We also need to teach them to understand the language for a range of teacher classroom functions. This language is not usually taught in the coursebook. When we plan tasks and activities we need to think about what language the learners need to do the tasks. If learners do not know how to ask for an explanation or clarification, they will use their **L1**.

**FOLLOW-UP ACTIVITIES** *(See page 174 for answers)*

1 Here are eight examples of learner language. Which function does each one express?

A Can you say that again, please?
B I don't have the same answer.
C See you tomorrow.
D Is it page 25 or 35?
E What do you think?
F Yes, I totally agree with you.
G Well, I think this is the best answer.
H Hi!

2 Each of the following sets of exponents A–D expresses one function of learners' language. Which function does each set express?

| A<br>How about starting with number five?<br>Let's do this together.<br>Why don't we ask one of the other groups? | B<br>Can you give an example for number 4?<br>Can I use this word to talk about myself?<br>Does this mean the same thing? |
|---|---|
| C<br>It's great to see you again.<br>How are you?<br>Good morning. | D<br>My answer's the same as yours.<br>Yes, that's right.<br>That's my opinion, too. |

**REFLECTION**

Think about these comments from teachers. Which do you agree with and why?
1 I don't think learners need English for classroom functions. They can use their L1.
2 My learners usually use their L1 when they work in groups and when they ask me questions. I don't think they know how to say these things in English.
3 I put examples of appropriate language for classroom functions on the walls of my classroom to prompt my learners.

## DISCOVERY ACTIVITIES

1  If you teach children, have a look at the examples of classroom language for young learners on pages 17–19 of *Teaching English to Children* by Wendy Scott and Lisbeth Ytreberg, Pearson Education Ltd 1990.
2  Choose two functions of learner language. In your TKT portfolio, list four examples of exponents of appropriate language your learners could use for each one.
3  Use an activity from this website with your learners:
   http://www.learnenglish.org.uk/welcome_english.html
   Make sure they are working in pairs or threes and listen to the language they use as they work. Which language functions did they need to do the activity?
4  Use the *TKT Glossary* to find the meaning of these terms: *hesitate, respond*.

**TKT practice task** *(See page 176 for answers)*

For questions 1-5, look at the situations and three possible functions. Choose the correct option A, B or C.

1  A learner does not hear the instructions the teacher gives. He needs to:
   A  ask for repetition.
   B  express agreement.
   C  offer an opinion.
2  A learner does not understand the meaning of a new word. She needs to:
   A  express doubt.
   B  give advice.
   C  ask for clarification.
3  A learner has an idea about how to begin a pairwork activity. He needs to:
   A  make a suggestion.
   B  make a comparison.
   C  express disagreement.
4  A learner thinks she has misunderstood a word. She needs to:
   A  give an example.
   B  check meaning.
   C  ask for an opinion.
5  A learner wants to encourage a shy learner in group work. He needs to:
   A  check information.
   B  invite him to speak.
   C  explain his meaning.

# Unit 28  Categorising learners' mistakes

## How do we categorise learners' mistakes?

Mistakes show problems either with **accuracy**, i.e. using the correct form of the language, or with communication, i.e. sharing information clearly. Learners can make oral or written mistakes. Oral mistakes are mistakes learners make when they are speaking. They make mistakes in the accuracy of, for example, grammar, pronunciation or vocabulary or in the degree of formality of the language they use. In written language, learners may make mistakes, for example, in grammar, spelling, paragraphing, ordering of information or punctuation. Learners' mistakes can be **errors** or **slips**. Learners are usually able to correct slips themselves.

## Key concepts

*Oral mistakes*

Look at the following examples of learners' oral mistakes. There are mistakes of accuracy (grammar, pronunciation, vocabulary) and **appropriacy**. Can you identify them?

1  She like this picture. (Talking about present habit)
2  Shut up! (Said to a classmate)
3  I wear my suit in the sea.
4  Do you know where is the post office?
5  The dog /biːt/ me. (Talking about a dog attacking someone)
6  What /hæpənˈed/?

*Accuracy*

Examples 1, 3, 4, 5 and 6 all contain examples of inaccurate language.

- In Example 1 there is a grammar mistake. The learner has missed the third person *s* from the verb. The learner should have said 'She likes this picture'.
- In Example 3 there is a vocabulary mistake. The learner has used *suit* instead of *swimsuit*. The learner should have said 'I wear my swimsuit in the sea'.
- In Example 4 there is a grammar mistake. The learner has put the subject and verb in the wrong order in the indirect question. The learner should have said 'Do you know where the post office is?'
- In Example 5 there is a pronunciation mistake. The learner has used the long /iː/ sound when she should have used the short /ɪ/ sound. The learner should have said 'The dog /bɪt/ me'.
- In Example 6 there is a pronunciation mistake. The learner has stressed the final syllable of the word *happened*, making it into a three-syllable word when it is in fact pronounced as a two-syllable word /ˈhæpənd/.

*Appropriacy*

Example 2 contains an example of **inappropriate** language. Although Example 2 is accurate, there is a problem with appropriacy. It is rude to say 'Shut up!' in the classroom. The learner should have said 'Can you be quiet, please?', or something similar.

*Written mistakes*

As with oral mistakes, these can also be categorised into slips or errors in accuracy or appropriacy, or errors in communication.

Have a look at this story written by a learner. In the margin, there is a code written by the teacher to show different kinds of mistakes. Can you work out what the code means?

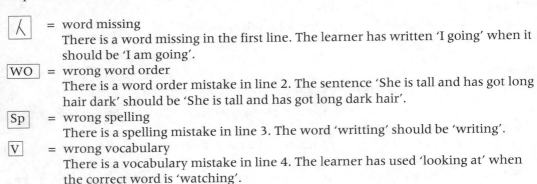

The teacher has used a **correction code** to indicate the types of mistakes in accuracy that the learner has made. This enables learners to make their own corrections. Here is an explanation of the letters and symbols:

⋏ = word missing
There is a word missing in the first line. The learner has written 'I going' when it should be 'I am going'.

WO = wrong word order
There is a word order mistake in line 2. The sentence 'She is tall and has got long hair dark' should be 'She is tall and has got long dark hair'.

Sp = wrong spelling
There is a spelling mistake in line 3. The word 'writting' should be 'writing'.

V = wrong vocabulary
There is a vocabulary mistake in line 4. The learner has used 'looking at' when the correct word is 'watching'.

P = **punctuation** (comma, full stop, etc.)
The learner has used the wrong punctuation in line 5. The learner has written 'Its' when the correct version is 'It's'.

Other common categories in a correction code are:

✓ = good sentence or expression            ? = Ask me (I don't understand)

prep = wrong preposition                     T = wrong verb tense

A = wrong agreement, for example *She like*   / = too many words

It makes learners lose **motivation** if we correct every mistake they make. We need to make sure our corrections are appropriate for the level and learning style of the learner and for the focus of the task.

# Key concepts and the language teaching classroom

- There are different reasons for the mistakes that learners make. For example: they may not have learnt the word or the structure yet; they may be using a word or structure from their first language by mistake; they may have been introduced to the language but may still need more time to process it or practise using it; they may have great difficulty making certain sounds; they may have writing or spelling problems in their first language; they may need more time to check and edit their writing. The reason why a mistake is made influences the way we correct it.
- There are different techniques we can use to correct oral and written mistakes.
- Mistakes can be a very positive aspect of learning. They show us that learning is taking place and that learners are taking risks with the language.

*See Unit 11 for the role of error and Unit 31 for correcting learners.*

**FOLLOW-UP ACTIVITY** *(See page 174 for answers)*

Here is another example of a learner's writing. Look at the underlined words and decide which symbol in the correction code you would use for each one.

In the past people used to travel <u>on</u> train or on foot. Now they usually travel by plane and by car. I like trains. <u>Train are</u> very <u>confortable</u> and you <u>can to read</u> or talk to your friends. Planes are fast and they <u>were</u> more expensive.

**REFLECTION**

Think about these comments from teachers. Which do you agree with and why?
1 It's very difficult to ignore mistakes in spelling or grammar. They seem to be the most important thing so I feel I have to correct them.
2 Learners think we're not doing our job if we don't correct all their mistakes.
3 It's easier to correct mistakes in accuracy than in communication.

### DISCOVERY ACTIVITIES

1 Try using a simple correction code for correcting learners' written work in your class. Remember you will have to demonstrate to learners what they are meant to do and show them what the different symbols mean. Write about your learners' reactions to the code in your TKT portfolio.

2 For more information on how to correct written work, have a look at Chapter 9, Section 3 of *Learning Teaching* by Jim Scrivener (2nd edition, Macmillan 2005).

3 Young learners love writing stories and this is a good chance for you to try out a correction code. Have a look at http://tqjunior.thinkquest.org/5115/s_writing.htm for some story ideas.

**TKT practice task** *(See page 176 for answers)*

For questions 1-6, match the examples of learner mistakes in written work with the types of mistake listed A-G.

There is one extra option which you do not need to use.

| Learner mistakes | Types of mistake |
|---|---|
| 1 She arrived to the station early. | A wrong punctuation |
| 2 We listened the music before we went out. | B wrong spelling |
| 3 I live in very cheap accomodation near the school. | C wrong word order |
| 4 This is a picture of my uncles sister. | D wrong preposition |
| 5 He hurt one of his foot fingers. | E word missing |
| 6 He wore a coat black. | F wrong agreement |
| | G wrong vocabulary |

# Part 2 | Classroom management

## Unit 29 Teacher roles

### What are teacher roles?

During a lesson the teacher needs to manage the activities and the learners in the classroom in different ways. This means he or she needs to behave in different ways at different stages of the lesson. These different kinds of behaviour are called 'teacher roles'.

### Key concepts

Which roles does a teacher use in a lesson?

Every teacher changes roles during a lesson. These roles will be appropriate to the type of lesson, activities, lesson **aims** and the level and age of the learners. At different times we may, for example, act as a planner, an informer, a manager, a parent or friend, or a **monitor**. For example, when learners are doing a **role-play**, one role we have is to make sure that they are doing what we want them to do. This is called monitoring. When we present new language to the class, our role is to inform and explain to our learners. Here are some roles teachers often use.

| Role | The teacher: |
|---|---|
| 1  Planner | prepares and thinks through the lesson in detail before teaching it so that it has **variety** and there are appropriate activities for the different learners in the class. |
| 2  Informer | gives the learners detailed information about the language or about an activity. |
| 3  Manager | organises the learning space, makes sure everything in the classroom is running smoothly and sets up rules and **routines** (i.e. things which are done regularly) for behaviour. |
| 4  Monitor | goes around the class during individual, pair and group work activities, checking learning. |
| 5  Involver | makes sure all the learners are taking part in the activities. |
| 6  Parent/Friend | comforts learners when they are upset or unhappy. |
| 7  Diagnostician | is able to recognise the cause of learners' difficulties. |
| 8  **Resource** | can be used by the learners for help and advice. |

There are certain roles that we usually use at certain **stages** of the lesson. For example, we are planners before the lesson and may be monitors during group work and pairwork activities. Sometimes we take on more than one role at the same time. For example, we might monitor and explain if a pair of learners is having problems with an activity: we monitor to see how well they are doing and we explain to help them do better. There are various names for the different roles of the teacher. The ones above are very common.

## Key concepts and the language teaching classroom

- We need to choose teacher roles which are appropriate to the age and level of the learners, the stage of the lesson and the purpose of the activity. This means we need to think about our roles when we are planning lessons and be ready to use different roles during our lessons.
- The correct choice of appropriate teacher roles will help our lessons run more smoothly and will make learning and teaching more effective.
- Some roles are more suitable for young learner classes than for adult classes, e.g. parent or friend.
- Our roles change at different stages of our teaching:

Before the lesson
- We are planners of our materials to make sure that the lesson is suitable for the learners and for the learning purpose.
- We are also diagnosticians of our learners' problems.

During the lesson
- When we are presenting new language or new vocabulary to the learners, we are informers.
- When we are setting up activities, we are managers.
- When learners are doing activities, we are monitors, diagnosticians, managers and a resource.
- When there are problems with discipline, we are managers and sometimes a parent or a friend.

After the lesson
- When we think about how successful the lesson was, what the learners understood and were able to do and what they had problems with, we are diagnosticians and planners. We look at our **scheme of work** to check if the next lesson is appropriately planned.

**FOLLOW-UP ACTIVITY** *(See page 174 for answers)*

Here are some examples of teacher language at different stages of a lesson. What do you think is the teacher's role in each one?

1 Teacher to a pair of learners doing pairwork: 'How are you doing? Is everything OK?'
2 Teacher to the whole class: 'We add *er* to make the comparative form of one-syllable adjectives.'
3 Teacher to a young learner: 'Does your finger hurt? Let me have a look.'
4 Teacher to the whole class: 'Right, everyone stand up and turn to face your partner.'
5 Teacher to the whole class: 'I think I know why you are having problems.'

## REFLECTION

Think about these comments from teachers. Which do you agree with and why?

1 I like my class to be organised and I like to be in control. I think my main roles are to inform and manage. That's what the learners want.

2 I believe that my role is to enable the learners to learn for themselves, so I involve everyone and try not to control the learners and the activities too much.

3 I teach young children. Most of the time I am more a parent than a teacher. But, in my opinion, the most important teacher roles are planning and organising, especially with children.

## DISCOVERY ACTIVITIES

1 Think about a lesson you have taught recently. Which of the teacher roles discussed above do you think you used in the lesson? Which teacher roles do you think were missing from your lesson? Can you think of times in the lesson when they might have been suitable?

2 For ideas on how different teachers manage their classrooms, have a look at section 2 in Chapter 1 of *Learning Teaching* by Jim Scrivener, Macmillan 1994.

3 Choose a worksheet which is appropriate for one of your classes from this website: www.smic.be/smic5022/teacherhandouts.htm
Use it with the class and then write in your TKT portfolio which teacher roles you adopted for the activity and why. What effect did they have on the learners and the lesson? Had you used them before? Will you use them again?

**TKT practice task** *(See page 176 for answers)*

For questions 1-5, match the descriptions of the teacher's roles with the roles listed **A-F**. There is one extra option which you do not need to use.

Roles

A an informer
B a monitor
C a diagnostician
D an involver
E a planner
F a manager

Descriptions of the teacher's roles

1 Before the lesson, she is ........... when she thinks about and prepares what she is going to teach.
2 She is ............. when she presents new language to learners.
3 She is ............. when she organises group work or pairwork activities.
4 She is .............. when she goes around the class and helps learners when they are working on activities.
5 She is .............. when she encourages all the learners to take part in the activities.

# Unit 30   Grouping learners

## How do we group students?

Grouping learners is using different ways to organise our learners when they are working in the classroom. We usually organise them to work in different ways during each lesson. The groupings we choose depend on the type of activity, the students and the **aim** of the activity.

## Key concepts

What are the different ways we group learners in the classroom?

There are two different ways in which the teacher can group learners in the classroom. The first is when she chooses particular **interaction patterns** for the learners, i.e. ways in which learners work together and with the teacher in class. They include open class, group work, pairwork and individual work, and the teacher to learner(s) and learner(s) to teacher.

In this table you can see examples of different interaction patterns.

| Teaching purpose: Why? | Activity: What? | Interaction pattern: How? |
|---|---|---|
| Review students' knowledge of vocabulary and/or structure and the topic or **context** | **Brainstorming** | 1  Groups: students to students (Ss ↔ Ss)<br>2  Feedback: students to teacher (Ss → T) |
| Check students' understanding of new vocabulary | Bingo game | Whole class: teacher to students (T → Ss) |
| Give students practice in **scanning** | Reading and filling in a **chart** | 1  Individuals<br>2  Pairwork: student to student (S ↔ S) |

In our lesson plans we usually use short forms for showing interaction patterns, for example 'T → Ss' rather than writing out 'teacher to students'. We use 'S' to mean one student, and 'Ss' to mean more than one student.

The second way in which the teacher groups learners is when she decides which learners will work together in pairs, groups or teams. The teacher considers the learners' levels, **learning styles**, learner needs, personalities and relationships with others in the class before asking learners to work together. She needs to think which learners will work together best in order to learn best.

# Key concepts and the language teaching classroom

When deciding how to group learners, we need to consider a number of different factors:

- The teaching aim. It is much easier to choose how to group learners when we have decided on the aim of the lesson and the aim of each activity.
- The learning styles of the learners. For example, some learners prefer to work as individuals, others in groups. Learners also have different personalities and find it easier to work with some partners or groups than with others.
- The ability and level of the learners. Most classes are '**mixed ability**', i.e. they include learners of different abilities. We can group learners for some activities so that learners of the same ability work together, and for other activities so that learners of different abilities work together.
- The personalities of our learners. Most of the time learners will work well together, but sometimes there are learners who do not work together positively, e.g. when one learner is shy and another is quite **dominant** (i.e. always talking and stopping others from taking part). We need to think carefully about how to group these learners.
- The class size. With a class of between 20 and 30 learners, we can manage pair and group work quite easily. With classes of more than 30 learners, pair and group work are possible, but need more careful planning.
- The previous experience of the learners. When learners are not used to pair and group work we need to plan how to introduce this way of working. We can start by doing short pairwork activities and gradually introduce longer and more varied groupings.
- The activities that we have chosen. For example, a discussion activity can be done in groups, a **role-play** can be done in pairs. But we can also choose to do these activities differently, depending on the needs of the group and the aims of the lesson. So, for example, a discussion activity can be done in pairs or as a whole class, and a role-play can be done in groups.
- The balance of interaction patterns in a lesson. A lesson where learners are doing pairwork for the whole lesson will probably not be successful: learners will become bored and there might be discipline problems. A lesson where learners are doing individual work for the whole lesson will probably not be successful either: learners will lose concentration and become bored. Equally, a lesson which is wholly teacher-led is unlikely to be successful: learners need a balance of different interaction patterns within one lesson.
- The **group dynamics** of the class. i.e. the relationships beween the learners and how learners will behave towards each other.

The first part of a lesson plan from a methodology book for primary learners is on the next page. In each activity learners are grouped in different ways: they work as a whole class, in groups and individually.

| Time | Teacher's activity | Pupils' activity |
|---|---|---|
| 5–10 minutes | 1 **Warmer**: brief revision of colours, using a team game. | Pupils stand in lines behind flags of different colours. The teacher says a colour. Pupils behind the flag of that colour put up their hands. |
| 10 minutes | 2 Bring in a goldfish or a picture of a fish to introduce the topic to pupils. Discuss the fish – what it looks like, its colour, its parts. Check who has a fish at home. | Pupils gather round the tank and say what they know about fish. They tell each other something about their own fish. |
| | 3 Tell pupils you are going to tell them a story. In groups pupils predict what the story will be. Get **feedback** from the groups. | Pupils talk together to try and guess what will be in the story. |
| | 4 Explain the activity, i.e. pupils have to colour their fish as the story requests. Give out colours and photocopies of a fish drawing. | Group monitors give out crayons and blank sheets. |
| 10 minutes | 5 Tell the first part of the story with actions and pictures. Continue the story with instructions for colouring. | Pupils colour in the fish drawings following instructions. |

(adapted from *Children Learning English* by Jayne Moon, Macmillan 2000)

The interaction patterns in the lesson are:

- Activity 1: two large groups/teams
- Activities 2, 3 and 4: whole class and groups. In Activities 2 and 3 the teacher is working with the whole class. The teacher then divides the pupils into groups for the prediction activity.
- Activity 5: individual work. In this activity the teacher is telling the story and the pupils are working on their own, listening and colouring.

*See Unit 13 for more information on learning styles and other learner characteristics.*

## FOLLOW-UP ACTIVITY  *(See page 175 for answers)*

Here is the second part of the same lesson. For each activity, identify the interaction patterns and their purpose for the stage of the lesson.

| Time | Teacher's activity | Pupils' activity |
|---|---|---|
| 5 minutes | 6 Get the pupils to compare drawings. | Pupils compare drawings in pairs. |
| 5 minutes | 7 Class feedback. Elicit from different learners the colours of the little fish. Use sentence prompts, e.g. *His face is …* | Pupils talk about the colours of the fish to the whole class, e.g. *His face is …* |
| 5 minutes | 8 Ask pupils what they thought about the story, in L1 if necessary. Ask whether the big fish was right not to give the little fish colour for his lips. | Pupils give their opinions to the class. |

(adapted from *Children Learning English* by Jayne Moon, Macmillan 2000)

## REFLECTION

Which of the following statements do you agree with and why?
1  I try to have a balance of different interaction patterns in a lesson.
2  It's best to separate weak/strong or shy/dominant learners into different groups or pairs.
3  The age of learners that I teach makes some interaction patterns difficult.
4  My learners don't like group work, so I don't do it.
5  When learners work in pairs or groups, they have more opportunities to speak than when they work alone.

## DISCOVERY ACTIVITIES

1  Try out some different groupings and interaction patterns and write up the results in your TKT portfolio.
2  You will find some useful information on grouping young learners in Chapters 7 and 8 of *Children Learning English* by Jayne Moon, Macmillan 2000.
3  For more information on practical aspects of grouping and interaction patterns, have a look at Module 16 of *A Course in Language Teaching* by Penny Ur, Cambridge University Press 1996.

**TKT practice task** *(See page 176 for answers)*

For questions 1-6, match the different activities with the most suitable interaction patterns listed **A**, **B** or **C**.

### Interaction patterns

A  pair or group work
B  individual work
C  whole-class work

### Activities

1  Learners do an information-gap activity with two sets of information.
2  Learners write their own stories.
3  Learners decide together how to report their conclusions to the rest of the class.
4  All the learners act out a play for the parents.
5  Learners do a written test.
6  Learners take part in a choral drill.

# Unit 31   Correcting learners

## How do we correct learners?

When we correct learners we show them that something is wrong and that they have made a mistake. We may also show them how to put their mistake right. When learners make mistakes in speaking or writing, we correct these mistakes in different ways. We use oral correction techniques to correct oral mistakes and written correction techniques to correct written mistakes. We also use different techniques when we correct different kinds of mistakes, i.e. **errors** or **slips**.

## Key concepts

What ways can you think of for correcting learners' oral and written mistakes?

*Oral correction*

Here are some ways that we can correct oral mistakes:

1  Drawing a **time line** on the board. Time lines show learners the relationship between the use of a verb tense and time. This technique is particularly useful for mistakes such as 'I have seen that film two weeks ago'. The time line to show this mistake might look like this.

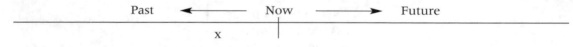

x = two weeks ago

This shows learners that, because the event is in the past and the time is specified, they cannot use the present perfect. The correct sentence is 'I saw that film two weeks ago'.

2  Finger correction. This shows learners where they have made a mistake. We show one hand to the class and point to each finger in turn as we say each word in the sentence. One finger is usually used for each word. This technique is particularly useful when learners have left out a word or when we want them to use a **contraction**, for example *I'm working* rather than *I am working*. We bring two fingers together to show that we want them to bring the two words together.

3  **Gestures** and/or **facial expressions** are useful when we do not want to interrupt learners too much, but still want to show them that they have made a slip. A worried look from the teacher can indicate to learners that there is a problem. It is possible to use many different gestures or facial expressions. The ones you use will depend on what is appropriate for your culture and your teaching situation.

4  **Phonemic symbols**. Pointing to phonemic symbols  is helpful when learners make pronunciation mistakes, for example using a long vowel /uː/when they should have used a short one /ʊ/, or when they mispronounce a consonant. You can only use this technique with learners who are familiar with the relevant phonemic symbols.

152

5 **Echo correcting** means repeating. Repeating what a learner says with rising **intonation** will show the learner that there is a mistake somewhere. You will find this technique works well when learners have made small slips which you feel confident they can correct themselves.

6 Identifying the mistake. Sometimes we need to identify the mistake by focusing learners' attention on it and telling them that there is a problem. This is a useful technique for correcting errors. We might say things like 'You can't say it like that' or 'Are you sure?' to indicate that they have made a mistake.

7 Not correcting at the time when the mistake is made. We can use this technique to give feedback after a **fluency** activity, for example. It is better not to correct learners when they are doing fluency activities, but we can make notes of serious mistakes they make. At the end of the activity, we can say the mistakes or write them on the board and ask learners what the problems are.

8 **Peer** and **self-correction**. Peer correction is when learners correct each other's mistakes. Self-correction is when learners correct their own mistakes. Sometimes we need to indicate that there is a mistake for the learners to correct it. Sometimes they notice the mistake themselves and quickly correct it. Peer and self-correction help learners to become independent of the teacher and more aware of their own learning needs.

9 **Ignoring mistakes**. In fluency activities we often ignore all the mistakes while the activity is in progress, as the important thing is for us to be able to understand the learners' ideas and for the learners to get fluency practice. We can make a note of frequent mistakes and correct them with the whole class after the activity. We often also ignore mistakes which are above the learners' current level. For example, an elementary learner telling us about what he did at the weekend might make a guess at how to talk about past time in English. We would not correct his mistakes because the past simple is a structure we have not yet taught him. We may also ignore mistakes made by a particular learner because we think this is best for that learner, e.g. a weak or shy learner. Finally, we often also ignore slips as learners can usually correct these themselves.

*Written correction*

In Unit 28 we saw how we can use a correction code to show learners where some of their mistakes are and what kind they are. Other techniques for making written corrections are:

1 Teacher correction. The teacher corrects the learners' mistakes by writing the correct word(s), instead of symbols from a correction code.

2 Peer correction. The learners look at each other's work and correct it or discuss possible corrections.

3 Self-correction. The learners, usually with the help of a guidance sheet, look for and correct mistakes in their own work.

4 Ignoring the mistake. As in point 9 above, sometimes we choose to ignore mistakes that learners make.

## Key concepts and the language teaching classroom

- In the classroom, we use a mix of teacher correction, peer correction and self-correction. Sometimes we need to correct learners. Sometimes we indicate to them that there is a mistake and they are able to correct themselves or other learners can help them. Sometimes we ignore learners' mistakes. We choose what is appropriate for the learning purpose, the learner and the situation.

- The technique we use for correcting mistakes depends on the type of mistake the learner has made. For example, we can use echo correction for slips, and time lines for errors.
- We do not correct every mistake our learners make. We correct mistakes according to the purpose of the activity, the stage in the lesson, the seriousness of the mistake and the learner's needs. It is inappropriate to correct all the mistakes learners make, and it can make learners lose motivation. When learners are doing a fluency activity, correction after the activity would be more appropriate.
- Some correction techniques are more suitable for certain types of mistake. For example, finger correction is useful for pronunciation mistakes and time lines are useful for mistakes with tenses.
- Techniques such as gestures and facial expressions give opportunities for peer and self-correction. This is because we show the learners that there is a mistake but we do not correct it.

See Unit 11 for the role of error.

## FOLLOW-UP ACTIVITY *(See page 175 for answers)*

Look at the following pairs of sentences. Learners often make mistakes and confuse the meaning of A and B in each pair. Draw two time lines for each pair which clearly show the differences in meaning.

1  A  Cinderella danced with the prince when the clock struck midnight.
   B  Cinderella was dancing with the prince when the clock struck midnight.
2  A  I play tennis on Fridays.
   B  I played tennis on Friday.

## REFLECTION

Think about these comments from teachers. Which do you agree with and why?
1  When learners make mistakes it means that they are not learning.
2  It is better to correct all the mistakes learners make.

## DISCOVERY ACTIVITIES

1  Try using some different correction techniques with your classes and write up your reflections on their success in your TKT portfolio.
2  For some more practical ideas on different correction techniques, have a look at Chapter 12 in *Tasks for Teacher Education* by Rosie Tanner and Catherine Green, Pearson Education Ltd 1998.
3  Observe a colleague using correction techniques and make notes on the Observation Sheet on page 249 of *A Course in Language Teaching* by Penny Ur, Cambridge University Press 1996.

························································································

**TKT practice task** *(See page 176 for answers)*

For questions 1-6, match the teacher's behaviour with the correction techniques listed **A-D**.
You need to use some options more than once.

---

Correction techniques

| |
|---|
| **A** ignore the mistake |
| **B** use self-correction |
| **C** draw a time line on the board |
| **D** use finger correction |

Teacher's behaviour

1  You have used a correction code to show learners where they have made mistakes in their writing. You now ask them to correct their own mistakes.
2  You are working with a class of elementary ten-year-olds who are doing a fluency activity. One of the learners is talking to the class about her pet. She says: 'My rabbit eat lettuce.' You let her continue talking.
3  You are doing a controlled practice activity. One of the learners says: 'I have been working last week.' You show her a diagram.
4  A learner is repeating the instructions for an activity and says: 'Then we choose /triː/ (three) objects.' You just listen.
5  You are focusing on spoken language and the use of contractions. A learner says: 'I am going swimming tomorrow.' You want to show her where the mistake is. You use your hand.
6  An advanced learner asks you: 'Can you borrow me a pencil, please?' You ask him to think about what he has said and to try again.

·······················································································

# Unit 32    Giving feedback

## How do we give feedback?

Giving **feedback** is giving information to learners about their learning. Feedback can focus on learners' language or **skills**, the ideas in their work, their behaviour, their attitude to learning or their progress. Sometimes we give feedback to the whole class, at other times we give feedback to small groups or individual learners. The purposes of feedback are to **motivate** learners and to help them understand what their problems are and how they can improve.

## Key concepts

Think of three comments you often give to your learners as feedback. What do they focus on? Why do you give them?

Here are some examples of teacher feedback to learners.

| Example | Focus | Purpose |
|---|---|---|
| Oral: 'Well done. This is much better.' | Progress, language and ideas | **Praising** the learner and telling her she is doing well; encouragement. |
| Oral: 'Have another look at number four. There's a problem with spelling and I think there are more than two people.' | Language and ideas | Telling the learner there is a problem with one of the answers and that she needs to look at it again. |
| Oral: 'Let's look at the new structure on the board again. I think some of you have misunderstood how we use it.' | Language | Inviting learners to look again at language that they are having problems with. |
| Written: 'What an amazing story! You've used adjectives very well this time. Your work is much better this time. You have tried very hard.' | Ideas, language, attitude and progress | Praising the learner on her good level of work, and the effort she has made and in particular on one part of her writing (adjectives). |
| Oral: 'You've made good progress in all your work this month. Your written work is much more accurate.' | Language and progress | Informing the learner of her progress; encouragement. |
| Written: 'B / 70%. Have a look at grammar section 5 at the back of the coursebook and check again the difference in meaning between the past simple and the past perfect.' | Language | Giving a grade and informing the learner of what the problem was with her work and telling her exactly what she needs to review and how. |

| Example | Focus | Purpose |
|---|---|---|
| Oral: 'You all did the pairwork activity quite well but I heard too much Spanish and not enough English.' | Language, ideas and behaviour | Encouraging learners but also informing them that they did not behave appropriately during pairwork. |

We can give feedback to individual learners (individual feedback) or groups of learners (group feedback). When learners give feedback to one another, this is called peer feedback. Feedback can be oral or written.

Feedback can be linked to **formal** or **informal assessment** and can be given to learners in the classroom or during individual meetings. We can also write regular feedback in the form of comments, grades or marks on a learner's record sheet. The learner can keep this sheet in their portfolio or we might keep it with our records of their overall progress and achievement. We can use this feedback when we make our end-of-course assessment.

Peer feedback is useful for all learners. The learners who give the feedback reflect on the work their classmates have done. The learners who receive feedback are given information on how they can improve. The learners are often guided by a feedback observation sheet. Young learners, though, are not able to give very detailed peer feedback because they are not yet able to think about their classmates' work very carefully. Peer feedback can have a positive effect on classroom dynamics and can help to train learners in skills they need to become **autonomous**.

Learners can also give teachers feedback about the lessons, activities and materials. They can tell us when they like what they are doing and when they are not so interested in the materials or activities, or when they are having problems with the language. They can also make suggestions for materials and activities to use.

## Key concepts and the language teaching classroom

- Feedback should be positive. We should tell learners what is good, what they are doing well, what they need to do to improve and how. This is particularly important for weaker or less confident learners.
- We can give feedback in the classroom during an activity, while we are **monitoring** learners doing pairwork or group work or at the end of or after the lesson.
- During feedback we can revisit or **recycle** language that learners are having problems with.
- Learners will need training in how to give feedback to each other.
- We can organise small-group feedback sessions, where the teacher and the learners can give and receive feedback on the classes and on their learning.
- Feedback which is particularly personal or sensitive should be given to learners in individual meetings and not in front of the whole class.
- It is useful to give learners written or oral feedback after assessment in addition to giving them a score – to provide encouragement and guidance for how to improve.

*See Units 17 and 21 for assessment.*

**FOLLOW-UP ACTIVITY** *(See page 175 for answers)*

Here are some examples of feedback. For each one identify its focus and purpose.

| Feedback | Focus | Purpose |
|---|---|---|
| 1 You have sat nicely for the whole lesson. Well done! | | |
| 2 I'm not sure that's right. Can anyone help? | | |
| 3 That was very thoughtful of you to help the other group. | | |
| 4 This is great, but not all your work has been so good this month. Some of it was rather careless. | | |

**REFLECTION**

Do you agree with these teachers' comments about giving feedback? Why?/Why not?

1 My learners are only interested in the marks they get for their work. They are not interested in my comments. They don't even read them.

2 My group of adult learners are always asking me for feedback on their levels and want to know how they are doing in every lesson. I think it's very difficult for the learners who are making slower progress. They don't like it when I tell them they are not doing as well as the others.

3 When I get my learners to give feedback to each other, they just say 'That's fine' and don't say any more.

**DISCOVERY ACTIVITIES**

1 If you teach younger learners, try the feedback chat on page 111 of *English for Primary Teachers* by Mary Slattery and Jane Willis, Oxford University Press 2001. Note down what happened in your TKT portfolio.

2 For more ideas on how to give feedback, have a look at Units Three and Four of *A Course in Language Teaching* by Penny Ur, Cambridge University Press 1996.

3 Try introducing peer feedback sessions in some of your classes. Is it effective? How do the learners feel about this approach? Note down what happens and the learners' reactions in your TKT portfolio.

4 Use the *TKT Glossary* to find the meaning of these terms: *get learners' attention*, *one-to-one*, *seating arrangement*.

## TKT practice task *(See page 176 for answers)*

For questions 1-5, match the situations with the kinds of feedback listed **A-C**.

1  The teacher notices that all the learners are having problems with the new language. She notes the problem down and discusses it later with the learners.
   A  peer feedback
   B  teacher feedback to the class
   C  teacher feedback to an individual

2  A young learner has just finished talking to the class about his hobby. The teacher says: 'Thank you very much. That was very interesting.'
   A  feedback on language
   B  feedback on attitude
   C  feedback on ideas

3  A teenage learner has written a story for homework. The teacher has written: 'This is so much better than last week's homework. Well done.'
   A  specific instructions on what to do
   B  identifying problems
   C  encouragement

4  The teacher writes on the first draft of a learner's composition: 'Look at this website for more ideas.'
   A  feedback on grammatical mistakes
   B  instructions on planning
   C  help with using reference resources

5  The teacher is talking to a group of primary-school children at the end of a group work activity. She says: 'You talked a lot today and I was pleased to see everyone working so well together.'
   A  feedback on pronunciation
   B  feedback on behaviour
   C  feedback on progress

# TKT Module 3 | Practice test

A *sample answer sheet is on page 168.*

For questions 1-8, match the examples of teacher language with the classroom functions listed A-I.

Mark the correct letter (A-I) on your answer sheet.

There is one extra option which you do not need to use.

| Examples of teacher language | Classroom functions |
|---|---|
| 1   We don't say 'good in' we say 'good at'. | A   monitoring |
| 2   You two, how are you getting on? | B   eliciting |
| 3   What can you see in the picture? | C   correcting |
| 4   Once upon a time there were two boys. | D   greeting |
| 5   Practise the dialogue in pairs for five minutes. | E   setting up an activity |
| 6   That's all for today. See you tomorrow. | F   checking learning |
| 7   Good morning, everyone. How are you today? | G   narrating |
| 8   Can you remember the meaning of these words? | H   disciplining |
| | I   ending the lesson |

For questions 9-15, put the teacher instructions listed A-G in order. The teacher is telling some young learners how to make a sock puppet.

Mark the correct letter (A-G) on your answer sheet.

| | |
|---|---|
| 9   ......... | A   Now, take it off your hand and stick the eyes in the right places. |
| 10   ......... | B   Now your puppet is ready to use. |
| 11   ......... | C   Pick up the sock and put it on your hand. |
| 12   ......... | D   Next, stick the nose under the eyes. |
| 13   ......... | E   Put it back on your hand when everything's ready |
| 14   ......... | F   Then, take a pen and mark where you're going to stick the eyes and nose. |
| 15   ......... | G   Put your sock, your pen, the eyes and the nose on your desk. |

For questions **16-20**, match the teacher's instructions with the comments on them listed **A**, **B** or **C**.

Mark the correct letter (**A**, **B** or **C**) on your answer sheet.

**Comments**

| | |
|---|---|
| A | language not well graded |
| B | language not well sequenced |
| C | language too formal/informal |

**Teacher's instructions**

16 The teacher says to a class of beginners at primary school: 'You'd better finish quickly as we're really short of time.'

17 The teacher says to a group of teenage intermediate learners: 'That was extremely well done. I do congratulate you.'

18 The teacher says to a group of adult elementary learners: 'Do the exercise on page 52. Open your books and check your answers with your partner.'

19 The teacher says to a group of teenage elementary learners: 'Use scientific lexical terms to define these words.'

20 The teacher says to a group of adult intermediate learners: 'Prepare your roles. Get into pairs. Here are your role cards.'

For questions **21-25**, look at the following examples of learner language and three possible functions.

Choose the correct option **A**, **B** or **C**.

Mark the correct letter (**A**, **B** or **C**) on your answer sheet.

21 Can you say that again please?

    A showing interest      B asking for repetition      C greeting

22 I don't think that's right. I think it's number six.

    A complaining      B advising      C disagreeing

23 What do you think about this idea?

    A checking meaning      B asking for opinions      C persuading

24 What do you mean?

    A asking for help      B asking for advice      C asking for clarification

25 Is this another word for 'beautiful'?

    A checking meaning      B making a suggestion      C agreeing

For questions **26-30**, match the teacher language with the teaching activities listed **A-F**.

Mark the correct letter (**A-F**) on your answer sheet.

There is one extra option which you do not need to use.

| Teacher language | | Teaching activities |
|---|---|---|
| 26 Listen and repeat together. | A | playing a game |
| 27 What do you have for the first one? | B | starting a drill |
| 28 That's not quite right. | C | prompting |
| 29 Whose turn is it? | D | commenting on performance |
| 30 No, it begins with 'c'. We learnt it last lesson. | E | setting up pairwork |
| | F | checking answers |

For questions **31-40**, match the circled mistakes in the learner's composition with the types of mistake listed **A-G**.

Mark the correct letter (**A-G**) on your answer sheet.

You need to use some options more than once.

**Circled mistakes**

31 Last summer we went on a lovely holiday. (All family went)

32 together to a house by the sea. My (family is horribly enormous.)

33 There were twenty of us, so we rented (a really big house that was having)

34 enough room (for all of us, There were) my brothers and sisters,

35 my parents, my (cosins and their parents.) It was great!

36 We (had always someone to play with) or something different to do – it

37 was such fun. Then in the evenings (we cooked a big dish.)

38 We all (take it in turns to do) the cooking and the washing up.

39 Sometimes the meals were fantastic, but (some which were horrible,)

40 (especially when brothers) cooked chicken.

**Types of mistake**

A   wrong vocabulary

B   wrong tense

C   word missing

D   wrong word order

E   wrong spelling

F   wrong punctuation

G   too many words

For questions **41-50**, match the teaching actions with the teacher roles listed **A-F**.

Mark the correct letter (**A-F**) on your answer sheet.

You need to use some options more than once.

**Teacher roles**

A   planner

B   parent

C   monitor

D   diagnostician

E   manager

F   resource

**Teaching actions**

41   The teacher goes round the class in pairwork, checking the learners' speaking.

42   The teacher prepares a lesson that suits her learners' learning styles.

43   The teacher makes sure that the class is well disciplined.

44   The teacher speaks kindly to a child who is crying.

45   The teacher answers the questions that learners have about the topic.

46   The teacher finds out which topics the learners need to learn about.

47   The teacher tells the learners what the new words mean.

48   The teacher is able to understand what the learners' language problems are.

49   The teacher makes sure that all the learners are taking part in the activities.

50   The teacher decides before the lesson which learners will work in which groups.

For questions 51-55, look at the following incomplete statements about interaction patterns. Two of the options (A-C) in each question are appropriate ways of completing the statements. One of the options is <u>NOT</u> appropriate.

Mark the option which is <u>NOT</u> appropriate (A, B or C) on your answer sheet.

---

51 Pairwork is helpful for

    A  checking accuracy.
    B  practising fluency.
    C  encouraging shy learners.

52 Whole-class work helps the teacher to

    A  get everyone's attention.
    B  decide who will answer.
    C  train learners to help one another.

53 Group work gives learners the opportunity to

    A  learn from one another.
    B  get clear guidance.
    C  practise their skills.

54 Mingling activities allow learners to

    A  get individual help from the teacher.
    B  relax when speaking.
    C  have a change of pace.

55 Individual work allows learners to

    A  practise their fluency.
    B  have time to think.
    C  work at their own speed.

For questions **56-60**, match the descriptions with the correction techniques listed **A-C**.

Mark the correct letter (**A-C**) on your answer sheet.

You need to use some options more than once.

## Correction techniques

A   echo correcting

B   peer correction

C   ignoring the mistake

### Descriptions

**56** In a class discussion a learner makes a pronunciation mistake. The teacher does nothing.

**57** Pairs exchange posters and work with a checklist to guide their proof-reading of the other pair's grammar and spelling.

**58** A learner is confusing the pronunciation of the words *ship* and *sheep*. The teacher repeats what he says.

**59** One of the learners says *light* when she means *right*. The teacher says both words.

**60** The teacher records learners doing a role-play. Then they watch the video and talk about the mistakes in their groups.

For questions **61-65**, match the classroom management problems with the possible planning solutions listed **A-F**.

Mark the correct letter (**A-F**) on your answer sheet.

There is one extra option which you do not need to use.

### Classroom management problems

61  Some learners start walking around the class, pointing and laughing at each other's work.

62  Eight-year-old learners are working in pairs, doing role-plays of job interviews. They are having problems with thinking of what to ask and answer.

63  A class of 30 learners has just done a listening activity. As the teacher is checking the answers of every learner in the class in turn, the learners are getting bored.

64  Some adult learners are having a discussion. But one is very quiet while the others talk a lot.

65  The learners are doing a ten-minute individual reading task. Some learners finish after six minutes, other learners take 15 minutes.

### Possible planning solutions

A    Organise groups so that learners who work well together are in the same group.

B    Plan how to make feedback interesting.

C    Make sure learners understand the rules of behaviour in the classroom.

D    Plan extra activities for different abilities in the class.

E    Use routines to set up activities.

F    Plan an activity which is more suitable for the learners' needs.

For questions **66-75**, match the teachers' comments with the focuses of feedback listed **A, B or C**.

Mark the correct letter (**A-C**) on your answer sheet.

### Focuses of feedback

A    language

B    behaviour

C    progress

Teachers' comments

66 You used some lovely adjectives in your story today.

67 Stop talking.

68 Your work has really improved this month.

69 I am pleased to see you helping the other learners.

70 You have expressed yourself well.

71 Your mark in this test is worse than last time.

72 You are such a quiet class today.

73 That was very clearly explained. Well done.

74 I'm not sure what you mean.

75 Good, you remembered to put your hands up.


For questions **76-80**, match the terms with the comments on their uses for classroom management listed **A-F**.

Mark the correct letter (**A-F**) on your answer sheet.

There is one extra option which you do not need to use.

| Terms | | Comments |
|---|---|---|
| 76 Rules and routines | | A provide different ways that teachers and learners can work together. |
| 77 Interaction patterns | | B are useful when the coursebook is not suitable for the learners. |
| 78 Positive learning atmospheres | | C mean that learners know what is expected of them in class. |
| 79 Balance and variety of approaches | | D encourage learners to work autonomously. |
| 80 Supplementary materials | | E mean that there is something to suit every learner. |
| | | F help make learners feel confident. |

# UNIVERSITY *of* CAMBRIDGE
## ESOL Examinations

# S A M P L E

**Candidate Name**
If not already printed, write name in CAPITALS and complete the Candidate No. grid (in pencil).

**Candidate Signature**

**Examination Title**

**Centre**

Centre No.

Candidate No.

Examination Details

Supervisor:
If the candidate is ABSENT or has WITHDRAWN shade here ⬜

| | 0 | 0 | 0 | 0 |
|---|---|---|---|---|
| | 1 | 1 | 1 | 1 |
| | 2 | 2 | 2 | 2 |
| | 3 | 3 | 3 | 3 |
| | 4 | 4 | 4 | 4 |
| | 5 | 5 | 5 | 5 |
| | 6 | 6 | 6 | 6 |
| | 7 | 7 | 7 | 7 |
| | 8 | 8 | 8 | 8 |
| | 9 | 9 | 9 | 9 |

## Use a pencil.

Mark ONE letter for each question.

For example, if you think F is the right answer to the question, mark your answer sheet like this:

0 A B C D E F G H I

Rub out any answer you wish to change with an eraser.

1 A B C D E F G H I
2 A B C D E F G H I
3 A B C D E F G H I
4 A B C D E F G H I
5 A B C D E F G H I
6 A B C D E F G H I
7 A B C D E F G H I
8 A B C D E F G H I
9 A B C D E F G H I
10 A B C D E F G H I
11 A B C D E F G H I
12 A B C D E F G H I
13 A B C D E F G H I
14 A B C D E F G H I
15 A B C D E F G H I
16 A B C D E F G H I
17 A B C D E F G H I
18 A B C D E F G H I
19 A B C D E F G H I
20 A B C D E F G H I
21 A B C D E F G H I
22 A B C D E F G H I

23 A B C D E F G H I
24 A B C D E F G H I
25 A B C D E F G H I
26 A B C D E F G H I
27 A B C D E F G H I
28 A B C D E F G H I
29 A B C D E F G H I
30 A B C D E F G H I
31 A B C D E F G H I
32 A B C D E F G H I
33 A B C D E F G H I
34 A B C D E F G H I
35 A B C D E F G H I
36 A B C D E F G H I
37 A B C D E F G H I
38 A B C D E F G H I
39 A B C D E F G H I
40 A B C D E F G H I
41 A B C D E F G H I
42 A B C D E F G H I
43 A B C D E F G H I
44 A B C D E F G H I
45 A B C D E F G H I
46 A B C D E F G H I
47 A B C D E F G H I
48 A B C D E F G H I
49 A B C D E F G H I
50 A B C D E F G H I
51 A B C D E F G H I

52 A B C D E F G H I
53 A B C D E F G H I
54 A B C D E F G H I
55 A B C D E F G H I
56 A B C D E F G H I
57 A B C D E F G H I
58 A B C D E F G H I
59 A B C D E F G H I
60 A B C D E F G H I
61 A B C D E F G H I
62 A B C D E F G H I
63 A B C D E F G H I
64 A B C D E F G H I
65 A B C D E F G H I
66 A B C D E F G H I
67 A B C D E F G H I
68 A B C D E F G H I
69 A B C D E F G H I
70 A B C D E F G H I
71 A B C D E F G H I
72 A B C D E F G H I
73 A B C D E F G H I
74 A B C D E F G H I
75 A B C D E F G H I
76 A B C D E F G H I
77 A B C D E F G H I
78 A B C D E F G H I
79 A B C D E F G H I
80 A B C D E F G H I

TKT answer sheet

168

# Exam tips for TKT

- The TKT test is divided into three modules which can be taken separately or together.
- Each module contains 80 questions.
- The task types used in TKT are: matching, multiple choice, sequencing (i.e. putting things in the right order), categorising errors (i.e. putting them into groups) and finding the odd one out.
- Each module lasts 80 minutes.

*Before the exam*

1 Know and understand the necessary ELT terms and concepts well. Read the relevant parts of this book, do the Follow-up and Discovery activities and think about the points in the Reflection sections. Doing this will give you confidence and familiarity with the subject.

2 Look at the list of terms in this book and in the *TKT Glossary* (http://www.cambridgeesol.org/TKT). Make sure you understand them, because they might appear in the exam.

3 Don't just learn the meaning of the terms. Think about the ideas behind the terms and what they mean for teaching and learning, too.

4 Do some TKT practice tests to help you get familiar with the task types, and get used to working within the time limit. Remember that the number of questions in each module is fixed at 80. There is one mark for each question.

5 Have a good night's sleep before the test!

*During the exam*

1 Don't worry about your English. Remember that TKT doesn't ask you to speak, listen to or write English. You just need to read the test and shade (make darker) with a pencil letters (e.g. A, B, C, D) on your answer sheet. There is a sample answer sheet on page 168.

2 Quickly skim through the whole test when you receive it to get a general idea of its content. The layout of TKT is clear and simple and all the task types are of similar kinds.

3 Work through the test from question 1 to question 80 if you can. In this way, you won't forget to do any questions. But, if you really can't answer a question, leave it, put a cross against it in the margin on your question paper, and come back to it when you have completed the others.

4 Read each question very carefully – both the instructions and the questions. Make sure that you understand exactly what you need to do and that you understand each question.

5 Sometimes the tasks contain extra options and sometimes you need to use the options more than once. Make sure you see and understand this information. It makes a difference to how you answer.

6 When you answer matching tasks, tick each option when you are confident it is the right answer to a question. This helps you to see which options are left for the other questions.

7 Don't forget to transfer your answers to the answer sheet and make sure you have answered the question you mean to answer. For example, don't write your answer to question 20 in the place for answer 19, and don't shade letter A when you mean to shade letter B.

8 In the matching tasks, if you feel unsure of an answer to one question, go to the next question, then the next, etc. You may find that, at the end of the task, the answer to your problem question then becomes clear.

9 Don't spend too long on any one part of the test. If you do, you will spoil your chances on the other parts of the test. Divide your time equally across all the questions. Leave five minutes at the end of the test to check your answers.

10 If you are getting too worried to answer properly, take a very short break. Relax.

**Good luck!**

# Answer key for Follow-up activities

## Unit 1

1  nouns: *box, walk, well, water*
   verbs: *box, walk, decide, water*
   adjectives: *younger, well, clever*
   adverbs: *well*
   determiners: *all*
   prepositions: *during*
   pronouns: *we, herself*
   conjunctions: *because, though*
   exclamations: *wow*
   N.B. Some of these words can operate as different parts of speech, e.g. *box* and *water* can be verbs, *walk* can be a noun, *well* can be an adjective, *all* can be a pronoun.

2  newer, newest, news, newly, renew, renewal; impossible, impossibly, impossibility, possibly, possibility; running, runner, runs, runny

## UNIT 2

1  A lexical sets  B antonyms  C collocations
   D synonyms  E compound words  F words with suffixes  G words with prefixes

2  A denotations  B synonyms  C antonyms  D lexical sets  E prefix + base word  F base word + suffix
   G compound words  H collocations

## UNIT 3

2  *book*: 3 phonemes /b/ /ʊ/ /k/
   *flashcard*: 7 phonemes /f/ /l/ /æ/ /ʃ/ /k/ /ɑː/ /d/
   *number*: 5 phonemes /n/ /ʌ/ /m/ /b/ /ə/
   *thirteen*: 5 phonemes /θ/ /ɜː/ /t/ /iː/ /n/
   *morning*: 5 phonemes /m/ /ɔː/ /n/ /ɪ/ /ŋ/

3  <u>twen</u>ty, <u>mon</u>key, <u>diff</u>icult, for<u>get</u>, re<u>mem</u>ber

4  *Possible answers*:
   My name is <u>Julia</u>, not Janet.
   Brasilia is in the <u>middle</u> of Brazil, not on the coast.
   The girl was <u>much</u> taller than her older brother. He was really <u>short</u>.

5  A ↘  B ↗  C ↘↗

## UNIT 4

1  *Possible answers:*

| Introducing yourself | A My name's X.<br>B I'm X.<br>C Let me introduce myself – I'm X.<br>D Call me X. |
|---|---|
| Suggesting | A Let's …<br>B Why don't we …?<br>C How about …?<br>D It might be a good idea to … |
| Asking for clarification | A Could you explain a little further?<br>B What do you mean?<br>C Sorry?<br>D Sorry, I don't quite understand. |
| Thanking | A Thank you.<br>B Thanks a lot.<br>C Ta.<br>D That was most kind of you. |

2  *Possible answers:*
   Introducing yourself: A:N  B:I  C:F  D:I
   Suggesting: A:N  B:N  C:I  D:F
   Asking for clarification: A:F  B:N  C:I  D:N
   Thanking: A:N  B:N or I  C:I  D:F

3  *Possible answers:*
   Introducing yourself: A and B
   Suggesting: A and C
   Asking for clarification: B
   Thanking: A

## UNIT 5

Before Reading: to relate the text to our world knowledge, and to introduce the topic
After Reading A: to practise reading for specific information
After Reading B: to relate the text to our world knowledge

# Answer key for Follow-up activities

## UNIT 6

1A  2B  3A  4B  5A  6B

## UNIT 7

1  contractions: *I'd*
repetitions: *sure, sure*
hesitations: *Erm, me, well, erm, er*
interruptions: *Would you be happy?*

2  The two learners are probably friends as they are
talking about quite personal things. It's not clear
where they are.

3  A gist  B detail  C specific information  D attitude

## UNIT 8

1A and B  2C and E  3C and E  4E  5A  6A and B
7C and E  8B  9D  10D

## UNIT 9

*Possible answers:*
A6 or 8  B5 or 10  C2, 3 or 5  D7  E9 or 10  F1 or 4
G2, 3 or 5  H2, 4, 7 or 8  I2, 4 or 5  J3 or 6  K6 or 8

## UNIT 10

| Acquisition | Interaction | Focus on form |
|-------------|-------------|---------------|
| 1, 2, 7, 8  | 2, 7, 8     | 3, 4, 5, 6, 9, 10 |

## UNIT 11

This conversation shows that the learners manage to
communicate with one another although they make
many mistakes. They seem to be experimenting with
language and really using all their knowledge of it to
get their message across to each other.

As this is a fluency activity, it would probably be
better for the teacher not to correct these learners,
and to make notes of important mistakes and correct
them after the conversation.

## UNIT 12

1  *Possible answers:*
Child playing with parents
• The child is getting individual attention.
• The learning time is not limited.
• The child is interacting with his parents.
• The child is enjoying communicating and
interacting.
• The parents can respond to the child's interests
and needs.
• The atmosphere is relaxed.

Teacher with class
• Learners cannot get much individual attention.
• The bell will ring after e.g. 30 minutes and end
the lesson.
• The teacher is telling the learners something.
There may be no interaction.
• The pupils may not be enjoying the lesson.
• The teacher cannot easily respond to each
learner's interests and needs.

2  *Possible answers:*
For Fatima, B is probably the best, because in this
way she could pick up English through playing. If
she went to England, she might feel lonely and
lost. Doing lots of homework would probably not
expose her to much language or help her use it,
but it could help her understand and remember
things learnt in class and make her feel more
confident.

It is hard to know what might be best for
Ricardo, as we don't know how he prefers to learn,
the level of his motivation or the time he has
available for learning. A or C might be best, or a
combination of these. B may help him to
understand grammar rules but won't give him any
practice in communication or learning vocabulary.

## UNIT 13

1  *Possible answers:*
As a reflective young learner who seems interested
in the target cultures of English, Pablo might learn
well by reading cartoon books in English, and
looking at websites about travelling in the USA. In
class, he may like time to think before he answers.
If his motivation continues, then in the right
circumstances he could be a successful learner of
English.

Pelin seems to have a problem with motivation.
She might respond well to learning in a
communicative classroom which has lots of pair
and group work. Her teacher could try and find out
why she is not interested in English. Her
motivation needs to improve to make her learning
successful.

Chen seems to be very well motivated. He
would probably respond well to studying the
English he needs in order to teach, to individual
work and possibly to grammar. He seems likely to
be successful in his learning if he has enough time
to learn.

2 *Possible answers:*
  A reflective  B kinaesthetic or group  C group or
  visual  D reflective  E auditory  F visual or
  individual  G visual or individual  H impulsive
     These activities could also be useful for other
  kinds of learners depending on the learners' age,
  learning needs and how the activities are carried
  out in class.
     All these activities could be carried out with
  both children's and adults' classes, depending on
  the character of the class. Some adults, though,
  might not want to do team running games, and
  discussing pronunciation with a class of children
  must be done in a very practical way.

## UNIT 14

1 *Possible answers:*
  Tatyana is a young learner who probably needs to
  learn in an active and sociable way. Gul has
  timetabling needs which mean he probably can't
  come to a regular class and may need to study a lot
  by himself. His course probably needs to focus on
  hotel English, on improving his speaking skills and
  possibly his skills in listening to people with a
  range of foreign accents.

2 *Possible answers:*
  A age; interests  B learning gap  C learning style
  D interests, language requirements for future
  professional needs  E language gap, future
  professional needs and learning goals  F age,
  learning style  G learner autonomy  H learning
  goals  I motivation  J motivation, learner
  autonomy

## UNIT 15

1, 3, 4, 7

## UNIT 16

1 Communication: B, D, F, I, K
  Accuracy: A, C, E, G, H, J

2 *Possible answers:*
  Role-plays and describing pictures could aim to
  develop either communication or accuracy
  depending on the instructions for the activity. If
  they ask the learners to use only certain language,
  they aim at accuracy.

A: speaking, writing
B: reading, listening, speaking, writing
C: speaking, writing
D: reading, listening
E: speaking

## UNIT 17

1  Picture composition/storytelling: probably use of
   vocabulary and grammar, pronunciation,
   linking, interaction, fluency, accuracy.
2  Listen and draw: probably listening for specific
   information.
3  Role-play: probably fluency, specific vocabulary,
   certain functions and grammar.
4  Interview: speaking – probably use of
   vocabulary and grammar, pronunciation,
   interaction, fluency, accuracy.
5  Gap/blank-fill: the form of the verb *to have*,
   accuracy.
6  Labelling: word and meaning recognition and
   possibly handwriting.
7  Repetition drill: pronunciation.
8  Project work: probably a range of reading skills,
   problem solving and speaking and writing skills.
9  Completing a self-assessment sheet: learners'
   ability to judge their own progress and/or
   performance.
10 Observation: Seeing what difficulties the
   learners have had in this area, and which areas
   may need further teaching.

## UNIT 18

1E 2H 3D 4C 5F 6A 7B 8G

## UNIT 19

1D 2A 4E 7C 8B

# Answer key for Follow-up activities

## UNIT 20
1 Lesson 1:B  Lesson 5:C  Lesson 6:A
2 A variety of pace: lessons 5 (video, role-play) and
     6 (project work, writing)
  B different interaction patterns: lessons 2, 3 and 5
     (pairwork) and 6 (group work)
  C receptive skills: lessons 1 (listening),
     2 (reading) and 5 (video)
  D productive skills (writing and/or speaking): all
     the lessons
  E increase of level of difficulty: lesson 5 (extract
     from authentic TV drama)
  F change of topic: lesson 4 (quiz)
  G change of language focus: lesson 4 (grammar)
  H lively and active: lessons 1 (flashcards), 4 (quiz),
     5 (role-play) and 6 (project work)
  I calm and quiet (with listening, reading and
     writing activities): all lessons except 5 and (with
     practice exercises): lessons 3 and 4.

## UNIT 21
1T 2F 3F 4T 5T 6F

## UNIT 22
1A 2A 3B 4B 5A 6B 7D 8B 9B 10C

## UNIT 23
Answers for these activities will depend on the
teaching material used.

## UNIT 24
*Possible answers:*
1 Intermediate upwards; oral fluency practice; little
   or no preparation; expressing opinions,
   comparative adjectives.
2 Intermediate upwards; oral fluency practice; little
   or no preparation; prepositions of place, reported
   speech.
3 Any level; listening, speaking and writing; teacher
   provides text; no particular language.
4 Any level; dictionary practice, exploring
   collocations and connotations; teacher provides
   words; no particular language.
5 Intermediate upwards; oral fluency practice; no
   preparation; question forms, expressing opinions,
   past tenses.
6 Any level; dictionary practice, extending
   vocabulary; no preparation; no particular
   language.

7 Any level; identifying word stress; teacher
   provides audio recording; no particular language.
8 Any level; intensive reading practice; teacher
   provides pictures and texts; no particular
   language.
9 Any level; practising writing narratives; little or no
   preparation; past tenses.
10 Any level; grammar practice; teacher provides
   sentences; no particular language.

## UNIT 25
1 OHP 2 language laboratory 3 realia 4 flashcards
5 blackboard/whiteboard 6 video 7 the Internet

## UNIT 26
1 *Possible answers:*
  A eliciting, correcting, conveying meaning,
     explaining
  B narrating, eliciting, prompting
  C explaining, narrating, prompting, correcting,
     eliciting
  D explaining, prompting, correcting
  E eliciting, correcting, prompting, checking
     learning
2 Language form: imperative, for example: *watch, cut,
  take*. Conjunctions: *Now, And, Then*.

## UNIT 27
1 A asking for repetition B disagreeing C saying
   goodbye D asking for clarification E asking for an
   opinion F agreeing G offering an opinion
   H greeting
2 A making a suggestion B checking meaning
   C greeting D agreeing

## UNIT 28
on  prep  wrong preposition (by)
Train are  A  wrong agreement (Trains are)
confortable  sp  wrong spelling (comfortable)
can to read  /  too many words (can read)
were  T  wrong tense (are)

## UNIT 29
*Possible answers:*
1 monitor 2 informer 3 parent and friend 4 manager
5 diagnostician

## UNIT 30

Activity 6. Interaction pattern: Pairs. Purpose: to get learners to check their answers with each other before they show their drawings to the teacher.

Activity 7. Interaction pattern: whole class. Purpose: to check learners' ability to identify the colours and to use the target structure to talk about their picture.

Activity 8. Interaction pattern: whole class. Purpose: to give learners the opportunity to talk meaningfully about the story and their response to it. A whole-class discussion at this stage is a good balance for the pair and individual work earlier in the lesson.

## UNIT 31

*Possible answers:*

1 A  Cinderella danced with the prince when the clock struck midnight.

| Past | Now | Future |
|------|-----|--------|

B  Cinderella was dancing with the prince when the clock struck midnight.

| Past | Now | Future |
|------|-----|--------|

♦ = strike   • = dance

2 A  I play tennis on Fridays.

| Past | Now | Future |
|------|-----|--------|

* * * * *

B  I played tennis on Friday.

| Past | Now | Future |
|------|-----|--------|

*

* = play tennis

## UNIT 32

| Focus | Purpose |
|-------|---------|
| 1 Behaviour | Praising a learner/learners and showing them you have noticed an improvement. |
| 2 Language, ideas | Telling the learner there is a problem and giving opportunities for peer feedback. |
| 3 Behaviour, attitude | Praising a learner/learners for the way they helped other learners in the class. |
| 4 Progress, language and ideas | Praising a learner/learners for the most recent work done but telling them that earlier work needed more careful checking. |

# Answer key for TKT practice tasks

**UNIT**

| | | | |
|---|---|---|---|
| 1 | 1C 2E 3D 4F 5G 6A | 30 | 1A 2B 3A 4C 5B 6C |
| 2 | 1F 2B 3A 4E 5D | 31 | 1B 2A 3C 4A 5D 6B |
| 3 | 1B 2C 3B 4 A 5C | 32 | 1B 2C 3C 4C 5B |
| 4 | 1D 2A 3G 4B 5E 6C | | |
| 5 | 1D 2C 3B 4F 5A | | |
| 6 | 1C 2E 3A 4D 5B 6G | | |
| 7 | 1B 2C 3G 4D 5E 6A | | |
| 8 | 1C 2B 3A 4C 5B 6A 7C | | |
| 9 | 1A 2G 3D 4B 5C 6H 7E | | |
| 10 | 1A 2C 3C 4C 5B | | |
| 11 | 1C 2A 3A 4B 5C 6A 7B | | |
| 12 | 1A 2A 3A 4B 5B 6C 7A 8A 9C | | |
| 13 | 1B 2A 3A 4C 5B 6D 7C | | |
| 14 | 1H 2D 3G 4E 5C 6A 7B | | |
| 15 | 1E 2C 3B 4A 5F 6G | | |
| 16 | 1D 2B 3A 4E 5G 6H 7C | | |
| 17 | 1E 2A 3D 4F 5C | | |
| 18 | 1G 2A 3D 4B 5C 6F 7H | | |
| 19 | 1H 2E 3F 4B 5D 6A 7C | | |
| 20 | 1D 2A 3E 4C 5B | | |
| 21 | 1D 2H 3E 4C 5A 6G 7F | | |
| 22 | 1H 2A 3F 4E 5B 6D 7C | | |
| 23 | 1C 2A 3F 4E 5B 6D 7H | | |
| 24 | 1E 2A 3D 4F 5C 6G | | |
| 25 | 1B 2G 3E 4D 5H 6A 7F | | |
| 26 | 1A 2B 3C 4B 5A | | |
| 27 | 1A 2C 3A 4B 5B | | |
| 28 | 1D 2E 3B 4A 5G 6C | | |
| 29 | 1E 2A 3F 4B 5D | | |

# Answer key for TKT practice tests

## TEST 1

1B 2D 3A 4E 5C

6C 7B 8A 9B 10A

11D 12F 13A 14G 15B 16C

17A 18B 19B 20C 21B 22B 23B 24C

25E 26A 27F 28B 29G 30C

31E 32B 33F 34D 35C

36C 37F 38A 39B 40D

41B 42C 43A 44B 45C

46A 47B 48C 49B 50A

51A 52B 53B 54A 55C

56F 57A 58H 59E 60G 61I 62D 63C

64C 65B 66C 67B 68C 69C

70B 71D 72C 73A 74E

75F 76D 77E 78G 79B 80A

## TEST 2

1A 2I 3D 4B 5G 6H 7F 8C

9E 10C 11E 12D 13B 14B 15F 16F 17A 18E

19B 20D 21E 22E 23C 24E 25D 26C 27A 28B

29D 30F 31A 32B 33E 34C

35B 36B 37A 38C 39C 40A

41E 42A 43D 44G 45C 46I 47H 48B

49F 50C 51E 52H 53B 54G 55A

56B 57C 58D 59C 60C 61B 62D 63D 64C 65A

66F 67A 68G 69B 70A 71D 72F 73E 74E 75C

76F 77A 78E 79D 80C

## TEST 3

1C 2A 3B 4G 5E 6I 7D 8F

9G 10C 11F 12A 13D 14E 15B

16A 17C 18B 19A 20B

21B 22C 23B 24C 25A

26B 27F 28D 29A 30C

31C 32A 33B 34F 35E 36D 37A 38B 39G 40C

41C 42A 43E 44B 45F 46D 47F 48D 49E 50A

51A 52C 53B 54A 55A

56C 57B 58A 59A 60B

61C 62F 63B 64A 65D

66A 67B 68C 69B 70A 71C 72B 73A 74A 75B

76C 77A 78F 79E 80B

# Alphabetical list of terms

All these terms are related to English language teaching (ELT). They appear in the *TKT Glossary* compiled by Cambridge ESOL and are first defined and discussed in this book on the page given below. Terms in *italics* are given but not defined on the page mentioned.

# Alphabetical list of terms

# Unit-by-unit list of terms

The following terms are used in the units, although they are not all defined each time. Terms in italics are mentioned only in the Discovery activities.

## Unit 7
authentic
connected speech
context
*develop skills*
extensive listening
facial expression
gesture
*infer attitude or mood*
intonation
listen for attitude
listen for detail
listen for gist
listen for specific information
meaningful
receptive skill
skill
stress
subskill

## Unit 8
accuracy
appropriacy
ask for clarification
connected speech
controlled practice
facial expression
fluency
function
interaction
interactive strategies
intonation
lead-in
productive skill

## Unit 9
goal
learner autonomy/
    independence
motivation
personalise
self-confidence
target language culture

## Unit 10
acquisition (noun), acquire
    (verb)
communicative approach
exposure
focus on form
grammar–translation method
interaction
pick up
silent period

## Unit 11
*cognitive*
developmental error
error
ignore (errors)
interference
interlanguage
L1
L2
overgeneralisation
slip

## Unit 12
*activity-based learning*
context
*deductive learning*
exposure
focus on form
*inductive learning*
interaction
L1
L2
motivation
personalise
pick up
praise
silent period

## Unit 13
*attention span*
auditory (learner)
autonomous
kinaesthetic (learner)
*learner training*

learning strategy
learning style
paraphrase
*self-access centre*
visual (learner)

## Unit 14
feedback
goal
interaction pattern
learner autonomy
learning strategy
learning style
motivation
pace
skill

## Unit 15
choral drill
concept question
context
contextualise
controlled practice
*definition*
elicit
freer practice
*icebreaker*
*illustrate meaning*
lead-in
learning style
less controlled practice
*lexical approach*
meaningful
personalisation (noun),
    personalise (verb)
Presentation, Practice and
    Production (PPP)
presentation (noun), present
    (verb)
restricted practice
*situational presentation*
task
Task-based Learning (TBL)
Test-teach-test
warmer

## Unit-by-unit list of terms

### Unit 16
accuracy
*chant*
communicative activity
controlled practice
drill
exponent
fluency
freer practice
grammatical structure
information gap
interaction pattern
*jumbled pictures*
*labelling*
lead-in
less controlled practice
multiple-choice questions
PPP
*prioritising*
*project work*
read for detail
read/listen for specific
   information
restricted practice
role-play
subskill
survey
task
TBL
true/false questions
warmer

### Unit 17
accuracy
achievement test
appropriacy
autonomous
assessment (noun), assess
   (verb)
*cloze test*
*continuous assessment*
diagnostic test
feedback
fluency
formal assessment

formative assessment
informal assessment
interaction
*matching task*
multiple-choice questions
objective test
*open comprehension questions*
*oral test*
peer assessment
placement test
portfolio
proficiency test
progress test
role-play
*sentence completion*
self-assessment
subjective test
true/false questions

## MODULE 2
### Unit 18
achieve aims
aim
*arouse interest*
consolidate
context
exponent
function
*give confidence*
grammatical structure
*highlight*
intonation
lexis
main aim
personal aim
phonemic chart
phonemic symbol
predicting
procedure
*raise awareness*
reinforce
scan
sequence
skill
stage

*stimulate discussion*
subsidiary aim
syllabus
teaching aid

### Unit 19
achieve aims
aim
anticipate language problems
assumption
interaction pattern
lead-in
main aim
personal aim
procedure
sequence
skill
stage
subsidiary aim
task
teaching aid
timing
variety
warmer

### Unit 20
aim
feedback
fluency
function
*guided discovery*
interaction pattern
pace
peer correction
Presentation, Practice and
   Production (PPP)
procedure
productive
receptive
recycle
role-play
scheme of work
sequence
set the scene
skill

*student-centred*
survey
syllabus
task
Task-based Learning (TBL)
*teacher-centred*
variety (noun), vary (verb)

## Unit 21
accuracy
achievement test
assessment
error
feedback
formal/informal assessment
intonation
matching task
monitor
motivation
multiple-choice questions
objective test
procedure
productive skill
proficiency test
progress test
receptive skill
stress
subskill
true/false questions

## Unit 22
anticipate language problems
collocation
dictionary, monolingual/
    bilingual
error
grammatical structure
interference
L1
language awareness
reference materials
resource
skill
supplementary materials

task
teacher's book
timing
worksheet

## Unit 23
activity book
adapt
class profile
context
diagnostic test
dialogue
interaction pattern
mingle
pace
personalised
present
realia
role-play
sequence
skill
supplementary materials
tapescript
task
teacher's book
variety
warmer
workbook

## Unit 24
adapt
aim
authentic material
communicative activity
context
extensive reading
feedback
grade (language)
graded reader
grammatical structure
motivation
procedure
resource
scheme of work
sequence

skill
supplementary materials
syllabus
task
variety

## Unit 25
chart
context
*crossword puzzle*
dialogue
elicit
extensive listening
facial expression
feedback
flashcard
*flipchart*
gesture
grammatical structure
information gap
language laboratory
*leaflet*
lexical set
lexis
main aim
mime
monitor
overhead projector
phonemic chart
phonemic symbol
predicting
present
procedure
puppet
realia
resource
sequence
skill
subsidiary aim
teaching aid
transparency
verb
*video clip*
visual aid
wallchart

## Unit-by-unit list of terms

MODULE 3

**Unit 26**
concept question
convey meaning
*define*
elicit
grade language
instruct
L1
*model*
mime
narrate
*nominate*
present
prompt
realia
sequence

**Unit 27**
ask for clarification
function
*hesitate*
interact
L1
*respond*
stage

**Unit 28**
accuracy
appropriacy
correction code

error
inappropriate
motivation
punctuation
slip

**Unit 29**
aim
monitor
resource
role-play
routine
scheme of work
stage
variety

**Unit 30**
aim
brainstorm
chart
context
dominant
feedback
group dynamics
interaction pattern
learning style
mixed ability
role-play
scan
warmer

**Unit 31**
contraction
echo correct
error
facial expression
fluency
gesture
ignore (errors)
intonation
peer correction
phonemic symbol
self-correction
slip
time line

**Unit 32**
autonomous
feedback
formal assessment
*get students' attention*
informal assessment
monitor
motivate
*one-to-one*
praise
recycle
*seating arrangement*
skill

# Phonemic symbols

Here is a list of phonemic symbols taken from the IPA (International Phonetic Alphabet) which show the sounds of British English.

VOWEL SOUNDS

| **Short vowels** | **Long vowels** | **Diphthongs** |
|---|---|---|
| ɪ as in p**i**t | iː as in s**ee** | eɪ as in d**a**y |
| e as in w**e**t | ɑː as in **ar**m | aɪ as in m**y** |
| æ as in c**a**t | ɔː as in s**aw** | ɔɪ as in b**oy** |
| ʌ as in r**u**n | uː as in t**oo** | əʊ as in l**ow** |
| ɒ as in h**o**t | ɜː as in h**er** | aʊ as in h**ow** |
| ʊ as in p**u**t | | ɪə as in n**ear** |
| ə as in **a**go | | eə as in h**air** |
| | | ʊə as in p**oor** |

CONSONANT SOUNDS

| | | |
|---|---|---|
| b as in **b**ee | n as in **n**ose | dʒ as in **g**eneral |
| d as in **d**o | p as in **p**en | ŋ as in ha**ng** |
| f as in **f**at | r as in **r**ed | ð as in **th**at |
| g as in **g**o | s as in **s**un | θ as in **th**in |
| h as in **h**at | t as in **t**en | ʃ as in **sh**ip |
| j as in **y**et | v as in **v**at | ʒ as in mea**s**ure |
| k as in **k**ey | w as in **w**et | tʃ as in **ch**in |
| l as in **l**ed | z as in **z**ip | |
| m as in **m**ap | | |

# Acknowledgements

The authors would like to thank all the people who reviewed a draft of these materials:

Mick Ashton

Jon Butt

Heather Daldry

Monica Mabel Gammel

Clare Harrison

Philip Prowse

Laura Renart

Amanda Thomas

Scott Thornbury

Frances Watkins

Their comments were very helpful. Our special thanks to our editor, Brigit Viney, for all her help and support.

The authors and publishers are grateful to the following for permission to use copyright material in *The TKT Course*. While every effort has been made, it has not been possible to identify the sources of all the material used and in such cases the publishers would welcome information from the copyright owners:

For the extract on p. 16 with permission of Macmillan Education from Simon Greenall, *Reward*, 1995, Macmillan Publishers Ltd; for the extract on p. 24 from *Super Goal 2* © 2001, by Dos Santos, Manuel, page 33. ISBN 970103340X. Adapted with permission of McGraw-Hill; for the extract on p. 27 from *Syllabuses for Primary Schools, English Language, Primary 1–6* (CDC, 1997), pp. 178–89 and for the extract from a listening syllabus on p. 31 from *Syllabuses for Secondary Schools, English Language, Secondary 1–5* (CDC, 1999), pp. 241–54, with permission of Education and Manpower Bureau of the Hong Kong Special Administrative Region [NB A new curriculum guide for Primary 1–6 has been recommended for use in schools in Hong Kong from September 2005]; for the extract on p. 39 from 'Ten commandments for motivating language learners: results of an empirical study' by Zoltán Dörnyei and Kata Csizér, published in *Language Teaching Research 2* 1998, pp. 203–15 with permission of Hodder Arnold; for the extract on p. 57 adapted from 'What do teachers really want from coursebooks?' by Hitomi Masuhara, published in *Materials Development in Language Teaching* edited by Brian Tomlinson, 1998, pp. 240–1; for the table on p. 98 adapted from *A Course in Language Teaching: Practice and theory* by Penny Ur, 1996, p. 217 and for the dictionary entry extract on p. 129, from the *Cambridge Advanced Learner's Dictionary*, 2003, p. 921 edited by Patrick Gillard © Cambridge University Press reprinted with permission of the publisher and authors; for the extracts on p. 150 with permission of Macmillan Education from *Children Learning English* by Jayne Moon, Macmillan Heinemann English Language Teaching, 2000.

p.50 top left, ©BananaStock/Alamy, top right, ©Powerstock photo library, bottom left, ©Martin Paquin/Alamy, bottom right, ©El Heraldo; p.55 left, ©Jim Sugar/Corbis, centre, ©Gian Berto Vanni/Corbis, right, ©Jack Hollingsworth/Corbis; p.59 left, ©Alan Oliver/Alamy, right, ©Jagdish Agarwal/SCPhotos/Alamy